LOOKIN[G GOD]
IN THE EYE

Encountering God in Genesis

———

TREVOR DENNIS

First published in Great Britain in 1998
Society for Promoting Christian Knowledge
Holy Trinity Church
Marylebone Road
London NW1 4DU

British Library Cataloguing-in-Publication Data

A catalogue record for this book is available
from the British Library

ISBN 0–281–05003–1

Typeset by Wilmaset Ltd, Birkenhead, Wirral
Printed in Great Britain by
Arrowsmiths, Bristol

Contents

For Antony and Bert

Preface

I squeezed the writing of this book into my duties at Chester Cathedral by means of putting occasional writing weeks into my diary, and then trying to keep them as clear as possible. I would like to thank my colleagues on the Cathedral Chapter, Stephen Smalley, Michael Rees, Owen Conway, and James Newcome, for their support, and for their unflagging patience. If my writing weeks got clogged up with other things, as sometimes they did, that was never their fault.

Lucy Gasson commissioned the book for SPCK, and gave me a great deal of encouragement in the early stages. Robin Keeley took over from her towards the end of the period of writing, together with other colleagues at SPCK looked after the final stages of the book's production, and was similarly encouraging. I am extremely grateful to them. The stimulus they provided and their reassurances meant more to me than I guess they realized at the time.

Without the love and constant support of my wife, Caroline, and our children, Eleanor, Sarah, Joanna and Timothy, I do not suppose that I would have started this book, let alone finished it. More than any others they gave me the security and freedom needed for the task. But I have also drawn a great deal of strength from our friends. To two of them, Bert Frew and Antony Mitchell, who have helped to show Caroline and me what living life to the full means, this book is dedicated.

Introduction

The intimacy of God is the great secret of the Church. It is one of the greatest truths the Church has to convey, yet for so much of the time it is kept hidden from its own members, let alone those outside the Church's boundaries. The talk of God that still dominates the worship and preaching of the Church is designed to keep God at a safe distance, and succeeds in doing just that. It keeps him closeted in a palace; and the vast majority of us do not even get to enter palaces, let alone feel at home in them. To make matters worse, God's palace is peculiarly inaccessible. It is in heaven, and heaven is not yet on earth. Because God is presented as an almighty king, we Christians are brought up to be deferential towards him: to bend the knee, doff the cap, touch the forelock. Because he is spoken of as our heavenly and somewhat old-fashioned father, we are taught to be polite towards him, to act as his obedient children, whose task is simply to discover his will and follow it. Ours is not to be overly creative, ours is not to take risks, ours is not to argue, and certainly not to complain.

How refreshing it is, then, to return to the book of Genesis in our Bibles, to remind ourselves of its stories of encounters with God, and to rediscover their daring, their mystery, their humour and their challenge!

This small book of ours is concerned with passages in Genesis where God appears on stage. Only in the last chapter, on the story of Joseph, are we called to remark upon God's absence from the scene, but that gives us a chance both to observe more closely how Joseph is portrayed in the narrative, and to reflect upon the book of Genesis as a whole and how the theme of God's intimacy is developed within it. Before that we enter the Garden of Eden, hear God's footsteps upon its gravel paths, discover that there prayer is as natural as conversation. We explore the depths of the tragedy of Cain and Abel, and realize that part of Cain's calamity is that he learns to pray too late. We see how Noah maintains an unnerving silence throughout the Flood, but how God is changed by it. We watch open-mouthed as Abraham tries to teach God how to exercise justice and how to be God. Twice we go out into the desert with the Egyptian slave, Hagar, first to hear her give God a name, and then finally to see her recover her dignity and her defiance. We are onlookers at Bethel as God comes down the stairway to stand beside the sleeping Jacob, then peer through the strange darkness at the river Jabbok as the two of them wrestle with each other through the small hours of the night. Only in the Moses stories can we again see God portrayed so close to humanity.

We look hard to see how the stories are told, how the various human characters are portrayed, and how God is depicted. We examine what they do, what they say, the silences they keep. We use our imaginations to fill some of the gaps in the stories, as the storytellers would have us do (for no storyteller tells us everything), yet we leave room for ambiguity and intrigue. We make connections between one story and another. We try to catch something of their suspense, their pathos, their tragedy, their occasional joy, the breathtaking surprise they all contain. We set out to enjoy them, hoping that the more we do so, the deeper we will enter into their mystery and their truth. These stories have the power to bring God out of heaven and down to earth, to remind us both of God's wonderful strangeness, and of his warm, unnerving intimacy.

To make discussion easier, each of the chosen passages is translated afresh from the Hebrew, and, indeed, whenever the biblical text is quoted a new translation is offered.

One important matter to do with the translation needs to be explained. God is often called YHWH in the Old Testament. This came to be the name above all names that distinguished the God of ancient Israel from the deities of the surrounding peoples. Written Hebrew has no vowels, so the letters YHWH are all we find in the text. Over several centuries of our Common Era, various signs were developed in the form of dots and dashes placed above or below the letters, to indicate the vowel sounds that should be pronounced. But the name YHWH was considered too sacred to take on the lips, and the custom had long been established of readers saying 'Adonai' or 'the/my Lord' instead, whenever they came across it in the text. So the vowel signs for 'Adonai' were given to YHWH, to indicate that 'Adonai' should be the word actually spoken, producing something on the Hebrew page that is nearly as impossible to pronounce as YHWH is on ours.

Religious Jews would still discourage us from trying to pronounce the divine name, and they have more than custom to support their case. For our most intimate God is beyond description, and beyond naming. God is essentially the unnameable one, as we remind ourselves in the fifth chapter of this book. A name, therefore, that cannot be pronounced seems only too fitting. It tells both of God's closeness, for it suggests he has come out into the open and revealed his identity, yet it preserves the sense of his otherness, his being always beyond our grasp and our telling. Most English translations of the Bible follow Jewish custom and substitute 'the Lord' for YHWH. The Jerusalem Bible and the New Jerusalem Bible vocalize it as 'Yahweh'. For the reasons just outlined, and encouraged further by current scholarly convention, in this book YHWH is left as it is.

1

Meeting God in the Garden

(Genesis 2.4b—3.24)

Why is the story of the Garden of Eden so compelling? Why has it caught the imagination of so many artists, poets, theologians, believers and non-believers through the centuries? Why does it still stir up such strong feelings in those who hear or read it, even in some of those who, in the words of the book of Job, only hear of it by the hearing of the ear?

No doubt, the reasons are many and various, and some more to do with how certain details of the story have been handled, than with the story itself – we only need to recall how often the woman of the story has been demonized, or turned into an evil temptress.[1] Yet surely these two chapters of Genesis – that tell of the making of a garden, of mysterious trees, and of a man and a woman and a talking snake; that present a tale of easy pickings and prospects of unremitting toil, of love and accusation, of the pains of growing up, of hopes of immortality missed for ever and life to be lived under the shadow of death, of union and disintegration, of loneliness and love, intimacy and expulsion – continue to enthral us because, within their small compass, they touch upon and illuminate so many features of human life, not just as it was lived by those to whom it was first told, but as it is experienced in every age, including our own. The story is, quite simply, a work of genius. We are hard pressed to find one of similar length in the Bible which is as brilliantly told as this, as sophisticated or as many-layered. It is like the ancient tels of Palestine, only instead of the strata of the debris of collapsed towns being laid one on top of another, here whole worlds, still fresh and full of colour, are to be found by those who patiently explore its tiny space.

1

We have still not said enough, however, to explain the Eden story's fascination. To do that we must also point to the way in which it speaks of God and his encounter with human beings. In that regard, it is, as we shall see, most unusual, indeed almost unique in the Bible. Only the next story, the one of Cain's murder of Abel, will talk in the same way, or nearly so. After that we will be left with but poignant reminders.

See first how God is described here, see what pictures of him are created by the storyteller! This God shapes a human being from the dust; he puffs life into the creature's nostrils; he plants a garden, takes the creature and puts him[2] there; he speaks to him, and without any prior formalities; he deliberates, and allows us to hear what is going through his mind; from the ground he shapes the animals and birds, and then brings them to the human being to see if they will cure his loneliness and provide him with the help he needs; he puts him into a coma, takes one of his sides,[3] closes up the wound, uses the side to build a woman, and brings her to the man to see if she will fit the bill. After that he retires from the scene for a spell, while a clever snake takes his place. When he returns, the man and woman hear him coming! He walks to and fro in his garden in the cool of the day, and with audible footsteps. He calls to the man, and engages him in dialogue, and then the woman also. He passes judgement upon them, and later, after talking again to himself, or perhaps to the other members of his heavenly entourage, he expels the couple from the Garden, and stations cherubim at its entrance to prevent their return, and a whirling, flaming sword for good measure. Before he does that he makes clothes out of animal skins for the man and woman, and puts them round their bodies.

This is an astonishing way of speaking, some of it unique in the Bible. In one important sense, of course, it is not remarkable at all. It is but an example of the storyteller's art. In stories we can come across talking snakes and mysterious, dangerous trees without batting an eyelid. Storytellers are adept at suspending our disbelief. They do it all the time. And when they introduce God as the main character, then surely almost

2

anything can happen. God can speak, walk, deliberate, call out, turn landscape gardener, potter or sculptor, surgeon or tailor, exhibit mysterious skills that defeat the imagination, and show compassion, bewilderment, anger.

Furthermore, as we will see, the Old Testament is full of this kind of imagery, frequently of the brightest, most imaginative kind, some of it drawn from, or inspired by the mythologies of the cultures surrounding Israel, much coming from the creative minds of its own poets and storytellers.

Thus we find God 'speaking' to plenty of other people, in plenty of other contexts. (Indeed God's 'words' are such a feature of the stories and poems of the Old Testament, that we come to take his speech for granted, and fail to recognize how extraordinary a metaphor it is, or even that metaphor is being used at all.)

We overhear God 'deliberating' before he creates human-kind (Genesis 1.26), before he brings the Flood upon the earth (6.7), and again when he contemplates the destruction of Sodom (18.17–21), or hear him 'addressing' members of his heavenly court at the start of Isaiah 40, or in the first two chapters of Job.

He 'walks to and fro' among his people in his tent sanctuary (see Leviticus 26.12; Deuteronomy 23.14; 2 Samuel 7.6–7).

The Hebrew verb *yatsar*, that the Garden of Eden story uses of him 'shaping' the first human being or the animals from the ground, is frequently applied to his creative activity, parti-cularly by the prophets. Isaiah 44.2, 24, for example, speaks of him 'shaping' Israel in the womb, and Jeremiah 1.5 has him say to the prophet, 'Before I shaped you in the womb, I knew you.'

In Psalm 147.2 he 'builds' Jerusalem, and again in Amos 9.6 he 'builds' his dwelling in the heavens, just as in Eden he 'builds' the woman from the man's side.

He 'plants' not only the Garden of Eden, but trees beside a stream in Numbers 24.6, or the 'vineyard' of Israel in Isaiah 5.2.

Though he may not put in another appearance in the guise of a surgeon, he, or rather she, is 'midwife' in Psalms 22.9 and 71.6, in Isaiah 66.9, and Job 39.1–4, while in Hosea 6.1 and

11.3, and in Jeremiah 30.17, he is Israel's 'healer'. As for his compassion, anger or bewilderment, there is enough of each in the Old Testament for whole books to be written on their subjects.

Yet some of the images of the Garden of Eden story are to be found nowhere else. Only in Eden do we hear the 'sound' of God's 'footsteps'. Only here do we find such near-explicit talk of his 'manual labour'. Only here is he represented as making things with what we might dare to call, if we were to push the language a little further, his 'bare hands'. Though he 'makes' things in the great poem of creation in Genesis 1, there the sonority of the language puts him at a greater distance from the things he creates. We cannot imagine the God of Genesis 1 dressed in overalls, or getting his hands dirty; with the God of the Garden we can quite easily. In biblical narrative, anthropomorphic language (language taken directly from the human sphere and applied to God) quite as bold and unashamed as this is only found in Genesis. Even there it is rare, becomes modified as soon as Eden is left behind, and in the long Joseph story in the final chapters disappears altogether.

There is a strange and peculiar intimacy between God and human beings in the Garden of Eden. In the middle of another garden, the one we call the Garth in the cloisters here at Chester Cathedral, is a large statue of Christ and the Woman at the Well, a meditation in bronze upon the haunting story in John 4. It is the work of a Liverpool sculptor, Stephen Broadbent, and to my mind one of the Cathedral's greatest treasures. The two figures of Jesus and the woman describe an almost complete circle. Their lower legs and feet are not delineated. Instead, where the feet might have been, their bodies join in a slender, smooth twist of bronze. The woman, whose body arches over that of Jesus, seems to spring from him and towards him. Their faces nearly meet. Their lips are slightly parted, as if ready for a kiss, while their hands are joined: she holds a bowl brimming over with water, and Jesus' hands are laid upon hers. It is a reminder, not only of John 4, but of that earlier story of Eden, and of its intimacies.

In Eden, it is true, God and human beings are not joined

together. They do not spring from God's body. Yet the brief descriptions of their creation put them and God at extremely close quarters.

Admittedly, the text of Genesis does not use the language I used earlier of God's 'bare hands'. It is more discreet than that, and leaves more room for mystery. The act of creating the woman in particular is one which defeats our imagination, and surely the storyteller meant to defeat it. Yet still, this God of Eden 'shapes' the first human being, and then 'builds' the woman. The first passage brings to our minds the picture of God bending low over the prone figure of his new creature, to put his lips over his nose and puff the life into him. True, the language of the story is again more cautious. It does not spell out, in the way I have just done, those stages of the act; no explicit talk of bending low, or putting lips over the creature's nose. Yet here, as with so much of the storytelling of the Old Testament, it is in the gaps left by the text, in the room left for our imagination, in what the story does *not* say, that so much fascination lies, and so much of the story's 'truth'. The truth of God's intimacy, the intimacy with which we were made, the intimacy for which we were made, also, is found as much in the gaps of this tale, as in its substance.

In the famous temple of Hatshepsut in Egypt, the one made so tragically notorious through the massacre of tourists there in 1997, a series of reliefs depicts the conception, birth and infancy of the queen. At her conception the creator god, Amon-Re, is shown extending the sign of life towards the nostrils of her mother. The God who walks in the Garden of Eden in the cool of the day comes closer than this. He breathes life into the body of the first human being, not with a gentle sigh, but, as the Hebrew verb employed at that point suggests, a vigorous puff. Between the faces of Jesus and the Samaritan woman in our sculpture in the Cathedral's Garth is a space no wider than two fingers' width. In Eden there is no space between at all. The contact between God and his creature is far more intimate than Michelangelo would allow in his famous painting on the ceiling of the Sistine Chapel, where God's and Adam's fingers so very nearly meet.

When it comes to the creation of the woman, the same intimacy is present. Once again there is nothing to separate Creator and creature, no distance between them. This is a hands-on God, a down-to-earth God, as we will not find again in the entire Bible, quite, except at the Jabbok. Only in the story in Genesis 32 of God wrestling with Jacob at the stream of the Jabbok do we see him so very close to another human being. Nowhere else at all will we hear the whirr of his sewing machine. Nowhere else at all will we hear the sound of his footsteps as he walks in the cool of the evening breeze.

Yet this is no oppressive intimacy. In the book of Job we find a man who speaks both of God's unbearable absence, and of his intolerable presence. In his agony and bewilderment Job believes on occasion that he can feel God breathing down his neck, and demands to be left alone (see Job 7.13–19). The divine intimacy of Eden is not of that kind at all. Just to prove it, as soon as he has completed the creation of the woman, and heard the man's surprise and delight, God retires from the scene, and leaves the Garden to the couple and to their new joy.

Most surprisingly – and this is surely one of the greatest surprises of this most surprising tale – the intimacy is not at once destroyed by the couple's disobedience and their taking of the forbidden fruit. For the sound of God walking in the Garden is heard *after* that point, and God's making clothes out of animal skins comes very near the end of the whole episode. Furthermore, in between those two details a dialogue takes place, which is not only the first of the Bible between God and human beings, but also one of the most remarkable.

And they heard the sound of YHWH[4] God walking to and fro in the garden in the breeze of the day, and the man and his woman hid themselves from YHWH God among the trees of the garden.

But YHWH God called out to the man and said, 'Where are you?'

He said, 'I heard the sound of you in the garden, and I was frightened, because I was naked, and I hid myself.'

God said, 'Who told you that you were naked? That tree whose fruit I forbade you to eat, have you eaten from it?'

The man said, 'That woman you gave to be with me, she gave me fruit from the tree, and I ate.'

Then YHWH God said to the woman, 'What is this you have done?'

The woman said, 'The snake tricked me and I ate.' (Genesis 3.8–14)

God in this story has not spoken to the woman before, and though he spoke to the first human being when he told him what he could and could not eat (see 2.16–17), and though the man broke into poetry to express his joy when God showed him the woman he had created (2.23), there has been no dialogue between them till this point.

What is so striking about this particular dialogue is the simplicity and directness of the language, and the lack of all formality. It seems so very straightforward, that it does not occur to us to call it prayer on the man's and woman's part, or if it does, we tell ourselves that prayer must somehow be more complicated than that.[5] Yet their speech in this passage is addressed directly to God. Admittedly they do not take the initiative. They speak in answer to God's questions. Yet theirs is no casual conversation, but a serious attempt to engage with God, and, in the man's case, to wrest from him some advantage. Could it be that here, most unusually, we have prayer presented, without any of the usual formalities, simply as conversation? Is this what prayer in Eden is like?

In the Children's Chapel in the Cathedral there is a prayer board for children to use. They write their prayers on bright slips of paper, and then stick them up on the board. They seem to understand this prayer of Eden. (In these few examples I have changed the children's names.) 'Dear God, My Grandma is in heaven. Have you seen her? Love Sarah.' 'To God. HELLO. Christopher.' 'To God. Thank you for having me. Love Rachel.' There is, of course, some formality here, that of the letter to a friend or relative. The man's and the woman's speeches do not even have as much as that. Nevertheless there is a refreshing directness and a profound simplicity in many of the children's prayers, which recall the prayer of the Garden, and from which we adults have something to learn.

Does this mean the man's and woman's speeches in the Garden are essentially childish? After all, the Eden story is about growing up. As we have seen already, the way the creation of the first human being is described makes us think of the foetus in the womb (see, again, Isaiah 44.2, 24; Jeremiah 1.4). After he is formed he is put in a safe place, where all is provided. Admittedly, God puts him in the Garden to cultivate it and look after it (Genesis 2.15), but it seems at that point in the story that if the creature wants something to eat, he has only to stretch up his hand and take some fruit, or, if he is thirsty, go down to the river and have a drink. There appears to be no need yet for the adult work of planting of the ground, or for the building of cisterns, and it is not even clear that Eden has such things as weeds! There is also for this child, besides the naming of the animals and birds, and the growing understanding of his own identity and uniqueness that goes with it, a loneliness and sense of incompleteness (2.19–20). But then, as a result of the second act of creation, boy meets girl, and we meet the surprise and the joy of romantic love.

At the time of their dialogue with God the human couple are, in fact, no longer children, but in the middle of a rather difficult adolescence! Duped by the snake, a creature cleverer, more sophisticated and cynical than they are, they have disobeyed one of the strict rules of their 'parent'. They have not been able to resist the delights of playing on the railway lines of Eden. Now they have learned their lesson, though it is not the one the snake promised them, nor the one the 'parent', in his fear for their safety, predicted. Instead, they have become aware of their sexuality and their vulnerability. Beginning, also, to realize what they have done, they are afraid of what the 'parent' will say. But when faced with the truth, they find it very hard, particularly the young man, to accept their

8

responsibility for it. The young man blames God for his predicament, and challenges his authority and competence: 'That woman *you gave to be with me*, she gave me fruit from the tree, and I ate.' (3.12) When God responds to the couple, and pronounces on what they have done, he will give them a glimpse of the adulthood they will soon reach in the harsh world outside the Garden, and leave them with words of its toil, its frustrations and its mortality (3.16–19).

In the earlier part of the story, when we had a child on the scene, there was no dialogue with God at all, no answering back, only God's telling, his giving permission and his establishing boundaries. Children, it seems in this story, are to be seen but not heard. The Bible as a whole neglects the bright spirituality of children, and these chapters of Genesis are no exception to the general rule. Only when the girl and boy approach adulthood, does dialogue with God become possible.

Their part of the dialogue, their prayer, is an unusual example of what is, in fact, the most common form of prayer in the Bible, that of lament and complaint. Not always is the complaint directed against God, but when it is, even when it is as sustained and as virulent as Job's, it is never condemned. God might argue with the substance, but he never denounces, or even so much as criticizes, the form. What is so unusual about the prayer of the man and woman is not its tone, but the complete absence of formalities, the intimacy from which it springs and which it expresses, and its implied egalitarianism. That last point we will explain in a moment.

The speeches of the young man in this conversation are laden with sorrow. 'I was frightened ... and I hid myself.' 'That woman you gave to be with me, she gave me fruit from the tree.' How different they are from his very first speech:

> 'Now this one, this time,
> Is bone of my bones
> And flesh of my flesh!
> This one shall be called "woman",
> For from "man" she was taken,
> This one!' (2.23)

9

How far the words of his prayers are from such welcome and such joy! They tell of damaged relationships, both between him and God and between him and the young woman. God did not make him afraid before. And his partner was bone of his bones and flesh of his flesh, not the cause of his trouble, as now he claims, and the fly in his precious ointment!

The young woman has less to say, and is not addressed by God till her partner attempts to shift the blame in her direction. This, alas, is typical of the Old Testament, indeed of the Bible as a whole. Just as it takes little notice of children, so it is hardly interested at all in the prayer and the spiritual life of women, and women will be centre stage in only one more chapter in this book. There is simply not enough material about their encounters with God for us to discuss. At least here, we can say, the woman of the Garden does not blame either her husband or God: 'The snake tricked me, and I ate.' For her it is the snake's fault. Perhaps hierarchy, newly established and observed since the taking of the fruit, prevents her from saying or even thinking anything else.

Nevertheless, for all the sadness of this dialogue, it still speaks of the strange intimacy of the Garden and indeed gives it further expression. At this point the young man and woman are still in God's garden. They are not yet expelled, and the cherubim and flaming sword are not yet in place to bar their return (see 3.23–4).

Those same cherubim and the sword tell their own tale. They take us at once into another world, not the uncertain one beyond Eden, in which we ourselves live, but the world of myth and religious symbol. In particular they take us into the realm of the cult and Israel's worship of her God. The whirling sword is without parallel in the rest of the Old Testament, but fire is frequently associated with the presence of God (think of the Burning Bush or the Pillar of Fire in Exodus), and if, as some have suggested, the wild movements of the sword and its flames are meant to suggest lightning, then that too, in Israel and among the Canaanites of Palestine, was a potent symbol of divine power. Of the significance of the cherubim there is no doubt. These creatures, part human

10

being, part lion, part bird, were the guardians of holy places in the ancient Near East. According to the traditions preserved in the Old Testament, their pictures, woven or carved, were on the walls of the tabernacle and the temple (Exodus 26.31; 1 Kings 6.29), two made of pure gold arched their wings over the throne of God set above the ark (Exodus 25.18–22), and two wooden ones, overlaid with gold and fifteen feet in height, guarded the inner sanctuary of Solomon's Temple in Jerusalem, and spread their wings from wall to wall (1 Kings 6.23–8).

Thus, once we are outside Eden and look back to its entrance, we realize where we have been.[6] We have been in God's innermost sanctuary! That is why he was 'walking to and fro'. For that also is the language of God's presence in his sanctuary, as we have mentioned already. Furthermore, that explains why we were able to 'hear' his footsteps, for being inside his sanctuary with him, we were at such very close quarters! In the end the cherubim can explain the strange intimacy of the Garden that is such a feature of its life.

But we, the 'ordinary' man and woman, are now outside Eden. That is how the episode ends. Human beings are barred access ... unless, of course, they happen to be priests or perhaps kings, playing their part in occasional ritual involving the ark of the covenant.[7] The man and the woman in Eden have no special status. All they have is their humanity. Inside Eden that is enough. Outside it is not. Outside priests and kings will take over, and claim for themselves the privilege of entering so deep into the presence of God. Moses, by the terms of the Exodus narrative, will show them the way, for he will enter 'the dense mist where God [is]' (Exodus 20.21), and will do so on his own. Moses' people will remain at a distance, and God and his holiness will be presented to them as highly dangerous, indeed lethal to the unwary.

We will by then be a long way from Eden, even if Moses' own relationship with God will remind us of it. Yet the story of God's garden will remain for the telling, and will continue to haunt the mind. It will present all who hear it with another vision, of a God who stands on no ceremony, and who does not stand for it either, a God for whose intimacy being human is enough, and with whom prayer is as straightforward as conversation.

2

In a Field Howling with
a Brother's Blood

(Genesis 4.1–16)

The man knew his wife Eve, and she conceived and bore Cain. 'I have produced a man,' she said, 'together with YHWH!' Next she bore his brother Abel. Abel kept sheep, while Cain worked the ground. (Genesis 4.1–2)

So begins the story of Cain and Abel, the one that immediately follows after the expulsion of the man and woman from Eden. So far so good, we might think, though already there are two details to give us pause for thought. One is carried over from the Eden story. There, in the course of the judgement he pronounces upon the man, God curses the ground (3.17–19). The man is condemned to a life of back-breaking toil outside the Garden, where he will try to scratch a living from a soil that will yield him only thorns and thistles. He will have to resort to eating wild plants to keep alive (if that is the meaning of 3.18b), and too soon (archaeological research would suggest by the age of forty) it will kill him. If we remember that judgement as we enter the story of the two brothers, we will expect Cain to have a hard time of it, and Abel to have to walk many miles a day to find adequate pasture for his sheep.

The second detail is more worrying still. Cain's name means acquisition, production, or creation. It is from the same root in the Hebrew as Eve's 'I have produced', and celebrates his birth in fine style, as indeed Eve does herself. In the context of this story 'Cain' could be very loosely translated Pride-and-joy. The name Abel, however, means something insubstantial, ephemeral, futile. It is exactly the same word as the author of

Ecclesiastes uses so often in his book when he declares everything 'vanity'. By the sound of it Abel will not last long. Soon
he will be gone, and there will be nothing to show for his
passing. 'Abel' in this story is Nobody. His birth is simply
reported. There is no cry of joy from his mother when he
comes into the world, even though the text would permit us
to think of him and Pride-and-joy as twins. He is Nobody,
counting for nothing. We will not hear him speak in this
story. He will be given nothing to say. Only once he is dead
will he make a sound, and then only God will catch it.

Eve and her husband leave the stage after the opening two
verses, and from now on this tale will concern just three
figures, Pride-and-joy, Nobody, and God.

> Now at the end of the season Pride-and-joy brought some of
> the produce of the ground as an offering to YHWH.
> Nobody for his part brought the fat portions of some of
> the first-born animals from his flock. YHWH paid attention
> to Nobody and his offering, but to Pride-and-joy and his
> offering he paid no attention at all. Pride-and-joy blazed
> with anger, and his face fell. (4.3–5)

The book of Genesis is largely concerned with family life, and,
once it reaches Abraham and Sarah, with one family in particular. Though a few altars get built and a few ancient sanctuaries
are provided with their origins, the religious ritual of Genesis
is conducted by male members of families, and not by priests.
There is only one professional priest in Genesis, apart from
those in Egypt in the Joseph story, and that is Melchizedek,
priest of El Elyon, the Most High God, in Salem. He features
in just three verses (14.18–20). There are no prophets either,
though at one rather curious point, Abraham is referred to as
one (20.7). Melchizedek blesses Abraham (14.19–20), God
promises Abimelech that Abraham will pray for him (20.7),
and Isaac prays for his wife Rebekah to have a child (25.21)
and blesses his sons Jacob and Esau (27.27–9, 39–40; 28.1–4).
Otherwise, until we reach the Joseph story, we do not encounter anyone who acts as intermediary between God and
another human being. Instead, human beings in Genesis can

enjoy direct access to God, without possessing any special status or exclusive expertise, and without the paraphernalia of any religious bureaucracy, though we have to admit it helps a good deal if one is male![1]

Yet still the appearance of sacrifice so early in Genesis is both startling and significant, although, of course, since they belong to the very first family, the brothers perform the ritual themselves, and need no professional help. There is little religious ritual of any kind in Genesis, and encounter with God does not depend on it. There was no ritual in the Garden, for all the echoes at the end of the later tabernacle and temple. Encounter with God took place entirely without formalities, and seemed to have something of an inevitability about it. To hear so soon of the brothers offering sacrifices is to be reminded at once that we are now outside Eden, where meeting God is more problematic and attempts have to be made to organize it.

Nobody and his offering are accepted; Pride-and-joy and his sacrifice are ignored. There is the rub, and there lies the heart of this story. There, too, is the point where fatal misunderstanding can most easily occur. Whether or not we believe we have encountered God ourselves, we want a deity whose actions are predictable and explicable, and free from arbitrariness or favour. We want a God of justice who is demonstrably fair. Any other kind of deity would surely be intolerable. We would never know where we were with him, nor how to approach him. Religious observance would become well nigh impossible. Thus, driven by sharp needs such as these, when we reach this point in the story of the two brothers, we presume that God's acceptance of the one and rejection of the other is fair and just, and understandable. We presume there must have been something wrong with either Pride-and-joy or his offering, or both, and something, indeed everything right with Nobody. We remind ourselves that Pride-and-joy's sacrifice of grain or vegetables or fruit comes from a ground which has been cursed. We notice the rather more elaborate way in which Nobody's sacrifice is described. We explain that Nobody was careful to choose the pick of his flocks for the offering, and even translate the Hebrew accordingly (the

Revised English Bible, for example, has, 'while Abel brought the choicest of the firstborn of his flock'). We assume that Pride-and-joy did not take such trouble to give God of his very best.

Yet let us look again at the biblical text, to see precisely what it says, and also what it does not say. We notice that it does not offer the comfort of such a tidy explanation. God is about to be concerned with what Pride-and-joy will do with his anger, but he will not refer to any flaw in his sacrifice, nor to any in Pride-and-joy himself that was present at the time of the offering, or before it. For his part the storyteller is careful to balance his rather more elaborate description of Nobody's sacrifice by referring explicitly only to Pride-and-joy bringing 'an offering to YHWH'. Of course, coming back to this part of the story from the end of it, from a field howling with a brother's blood and a Pride-and-joy who might seem to show no remorse for Nobody's murder, we can very quickly say that God knew from the start what kind of man he was dealing with, and therefore rejected him. But this again too easily lets God off the hook of this story, and results in our missing the point of it. For this story is concerned with what we human beings do, and what we might do, when confronted with a seemingly inexplicable God.

If the storyteller has given us any clue at all about what is going on, then it is in the names of the two brothers, the timing of their births, and the character of YHWH as it will emerge in the rest of Genesis and beyond. As Ellen van Wolde has pointed out, YHWH is the only one in this story to pay the 'worthless' younger brother any attention.[2] The God we meet in the rest of the Old Testament almost invariably takes notice of the Nobodys of this world, particularly when no-one else is doing so. Furthermore, the God of Genesis in particular usually supports younger brothers at the expense of older ones (think of Isaac and Ishmael, Jacob and Esau – who, of course, are twins – or Joseph and his older brothers). Maybe there *is* something wrong with Pride-and-joy, after all. Maybe he is the spoiled elder brother, the one who expects to be treated better by his parents, including his 'parent' God;

the one who assumes he and his gift will be accepted, but doubts whether that useless kid brother of his will be able to produce anything decent.

YHWH's rejection of him and his gift is designed, in that case, to encourage him to examine his assumptions about himself and his brother, to reassess his relationship with him, and to reconsider his theology into the bargain. If he assumes YHWH will pat him on the head, because he is his mother's favourite, and treat his brother as useless, like everyone else, then he had better think again!

Yet, if that is God's purpose, it fails. Pride-and-joy makes no sense of things at all. As in the Garden of Eden, we are dealing with human beings, or one human being, at least, who does not seem to have grown up, and with a God who is still conceived as parent. Just like a small child, Pride-and-joy is competing with his brother for God's attention and favour. Against all expectations, he loses out to his younger brother. He is not mature enough to work it out, or learn the lessons he is being taught. The curriculum is beyond him. The 'parent' is being terribly unfair to him. That is all he thinks he understands.

On one level, then, this tale is about the apparent arbitrariness of God, and the seemingly impenetrable mystery surrounding his activity, about the frequent unfairness of life and the seeming unfairness of God. That subject provides much of the Old Testament literature with its raw material. It is the central theme in many of the Psalms and is explored at the greatest depth of all in the book of Job.

So what does Cain *do* when faced with a God who makes no sense to him? And *what might he have done?*

We all know the answer to the first of those questions. He murders Nobody, and fulfils the dark promise of his younger brother's name. Unable, or rather not choosing, to take it out on God, who is for him the real culprit, the cause of his anger and despair, he destroys his brother, and leaves his blood soaking into the ground.

Before he acts, before anger turns to murder, God intervenes with a warning:

YHWH said to Pride-and-joy, 'Why do you burn with anger? Why has your face fallen? Surely if you do good, there is a lifting up. But if you do not do good, sin is at the door, the sin of lying in wait;[3] it longs to have you, but you must be its master.' (4.6–7)

As in the Garden, monologue comes before dialogue. Not until the fruit was taken did God and the young man and woman exchange speech with one another, speak and then respond. Not till things were spoiled did we hear the couple pray. Likewise in this story God and Pride-and-joy will not enter into dialogue till the deed is done and Nobody lies feeding the earth with his blood. In Eden, also, God's first speech to the child he had shaped from the ground was large with opportunity, but, like this one, contained some dark words. It gave freedom to eat from the trees of the Garden, then a restriction and a warning (2.16–17). The freedom was far greater than the restriction. Only one tree was forbidden; all the others were for easy picking. But the warning was a dire one, and spoke of death. The warning to Pride-and-joy is condensed in the Hebrew, and somewhat obscure. Yet it certainly holds its own terror. Pride-and-joy has a new enemy. He thought God was against him. He thought God was treating him as if he was worthless, like his brother. He was wrong. God's intervention is itself a sign that he has not rejected him, while the real enemy is not God at all, but sin. We have not heard of 'sin' before. There was no mention of it in the Garden. Now it is outside Pride-and-joy's door, and is out to get him, with a 'longing' for him as strong as the woman's sexual 'longing' for her husband in Genesis 3.16.[4] It is out to get him, as he is out to get his brother. It waits for him to step outside, just as he will soon ambush Nobody in the open field.

Yet there is freedom given in this speech of God's also, as there was in his speech to the child in 2.16–17. Sin may be dangerous, and very close at hand, but it is not invincible. It can be mastered, and indeed, Pride-and-joy must master it, if ruin is to be avoided. Though angry, bewildered and feeling rejected, he has not been robbed of choice. His feelings, for all their strength, do not compel him to act in a particular way. He is not their slave. Nor are the feelings themselves condemned. God asks of him why he is angry, but he does not pass judgement upon him for feeling as he does. The Old Testament writers in general had less of a problem with anger than we sometimes do, and God's questions are meant not to convict, but to help this young man grow up, face the anger boiling inside him and acknowledge its roots, and then deal with it in a mature and responsible way. He can *choose what to do*. That is one thing the speech is trying to make plain.

So what *might* Pride-and-joy have done instead of killing his brother? Calmed down at once, and shaken Nobody by the hand? Such a conclusion to the story would have seemed too easy for words, and certainly too romantic for Genesis, which looks the realities of human conduct so squarely in the face. No. But he might have hurled his anger at God, expressed his pain and bewilderment, and demanded a reason for the rejection of him and his sacrifice. 'What's wrong with my sacrifice? What's wrong with me? Why is my kid brother's offering so much better than mine? What's so good about him? He's Nobody, *Nobody*! It's not fair! *It's not fair!*' This is surely what he might have said. Indeed, the Old Testament, and this story itself, might suggest that is roughly what he *should* have said.

Had he done so, he might, of course, have arrived much sooner at the truth, and found there was no need for murder.

This tale is full of tragedy: the tragedy of a young man murdering his brother; the tragedy of his final estrangement from God and from the ground that gives him a living. And there is a third one, more carefully concealed than the other two: he turns to prayer too late. God's speech invited his response. It contained two questions. Had Pride-and-joy seized the moment and answered God at this early stage, had he let his anger out in words of accusation and demand, then God would have been able to respond, and there would have been hope, surely much hope, for both the brothers.

As it is, Pride-and-joy says nothing, but turns on his heel and goes away, with his anger still raging inside him. When he and his brother are out in the field, he leaps upon him like a wild animal,[5] and kills him. The dreadful deed is done, and Pride-and-joy and sin have their way. God comes on the scene once more with another question, and then, too late, too late, Pride-and-joy answers him.

> YHWH said to Pride-and-joy, 'Where is Nobody, your brother?'
> He said, 'I do not know. Am *I* my brother's keeper?'
> He said, 'What have you done? Your brother's blood is howling to me from the ground! Now you are more cursed than the ground,[6] which has opened its mouth to take your brother's blood from your hand. When you work the ground, it will not yield its strength to you. A vagabond and a vagrant will you be on earth.' (4.9–12)

If we had any difficulty recognizing the speeches of the young man and woman in the Garden in 3.10, 12 and 13 as prayer, then surely the dark cynicism of Cain's first speech here, 'I do not know. Am *I* my brother's keeper?', presents us with even greater difficulty. But prayer in the Old Testament does not need to be deferential. Indeed it often is not. Nor, to be prayer, does it need to be honourable, or speak the truth. It needs only to be addressed to God, to attempt to gain his attention, and to invite him to declare the truth.

In fact, this part of the story gives us the second, and in the narratives of the Bible, nearly the last example of prayer as conversation. Only Moses will engage God in speech as bare of formalities as this, and even he will not dare do it very often. And we have another example here of prayer of complaint against God. The accusation is veiled admittedly, and invisible in most English translations. Literally the Hebrew reads, 'I do not know. The keeper of my brother, I?' The final pronoun, the second 'I', is left to the end, to close the sentence, and gain emphasis as a result. We have tried to indicate that in our translation by putting it in italics. The emphasis both hides and reveals an accusation. '*I* am not responsible for my brother, parent God, but *you* are, and a fine job you've made of it!' That seems to be the sense of it. It reminds us of the young man in the Garden blaming God for giving him the woman, when she had given him the forbidden fruit, but, of course, it takes us far further into the darkness of human wickedness. Pride-and-joy, after all, has just murdered his brother. It is no time for cynicism. And his prayer contains an outright lie, as well as an accusation. It is no time for denial either.

Yet in the accusation, in the very complaint, lies the hope for Pride-and-joy. Not only is he starting to pray, he is beginning, just beginning, for the complaint is only made in the position of one word in a sentence, to face God with his truth. For all his dissembling, he is beginning to look at God, even if for the moment it is out of the corner of his eye. His dark words begin to reveal the bitterness which took him over when he and his sacrifice were ignored, and which drove him to murder his brother. He is beginning to take it out on God, as he should have done before. He is too late. He has already taken the very life out of Nobody.

The elder brother in this story learns how to pray, but not quickly enough. His prayer only begins its faltering way after he has committed the crime, and it only comes to fullness of speech once that sentence is pronounced. By then he has grown tall enough to look God straight in the eye. In great anguish he cries,

> 'My guilt/wickedness/punishment is too great to bear! Look, you have banished me this day from the face of the ground, and from your face I shall be hidden. I shall be a vagabond and a vagrant on the earth, and whoever finds me will kill me!' (4.13–14)

If we come to this speech from the Psalms, or from Jeremiah or from Job, we will recognize it at once as the mature prayer of lament and complaint. It starts with an ambiguity in the Hebrew, which we have left intact in our translation. It would seem from what follows that Pride-and-joy is complaining of his *punishment*, and the Hebrew term used can mean that. But it can also mean guilt or wickedness. Unless it does mean guilt or wickedness, he is still showing no remorse for the murder of his brother. And certainly in the rest of his prayer he forgets him, and concentrates on himself alone and his plight.

21

He makes clear to God what he has done to him: destroyed his livelihood, denied him any homecoming, put him in danger of being killed for what he has done, and made it impossible for him to look him in the eye ever again. This last charge is his response to being cursed. In the judgements he pronounced in the Garden, God cursed the snake and the ground, but he did not curse the man or the woman (see 3.14–19). But Pride-and-joy has heard the terrible words, 'Now *you* are ... cursed.' To be blessed by God is to find his presence; to be cursed by him is to be denied it. Pride-and-joy understands at once. Having just learned the art of prayer and its necessity, he knows he will never be able to pray like this again. Never again will he be able to look God in the face. It will be worse for him than it will be for Job. Job in his agony will batter God's door until his fists are raw. Job will claim that God will never answer him, but part of him cannot believe that, for why else would he continue? Pride-and-joy knows all hope of encountering God and his mercy are gone for ever. Job's wife calls upon him to curse God, and he does indeed come within an ace of it before he is done. But God never curses him. For Pride-and-joy it is different, and he understands the curse's terrifying finality. Of all the elements of his punishment, this is surely the most unbearable. It has about it the finality of hell.

Surprisingly, it is not the last word in this story. God responds once more:

> 'Not so! Whoever kills Pride-and-joy will suffer vengeance seven-fold.' And YHWH put a mark on Pride-and-joy, so that no-one who found him would strike him. (4.15)

There is undoubtedly a glimmer of hope here, though not perhaps quite where we might suppose at first glance. God's speech and action do not represent a mitigation of the punishment. He responds explicitly only to Pride-and-joy's complaint that anyone who finds him will kill him. He seems to ignore the rest, or to have nothing else to add to what he said before. Nor must we exaggerate God's compassion for the man, much as we might wish for a clear expression of it. The mark he puts on him is ambiguous. It will protect him from harm, it is true. There is some mercy in that, and a desire on God's part to avoid further violence and murder. But the mark will also brand him as a murderer, as one who killed his brother. And it is indelible. Like the curse it has a terrible finality. The little mercy being shown to Pride-and-joy is all he is getting. There will be no more where that came from, nor any forgiveness.

Does the hope lie, then, not so much in the terms in which God speaks to him, but in his speaking to him at all? After the curse, whose meaning Pride-and-joy was so quick to see, we might have expected his prayer to be received with deafening silence. In this story, however, the curse is not quite the end of things. The conversation is resumed, and conversation which seeks, for all its fearful limitations, to give some reassurance. Might God's speech, his speaking further to Pride-and-joy at all, mean that the man's reading of the curse is wrong? Might the curse, after all, not have brought encounter to an end, but just made it more problematic? His situation is certainly worse than that of his parents after their expulsion from Eden. But might it not be quite so hopeless as those words, 'You are cursed' would intimate?

Hell is the most hellish of all doctrines, and always has been. Some of us cannot believe in it and believe in God at the same time. It makes his love so small, and seems to spit in the face of the God we have encountered. And so we will clutch at any straw this story gives us, to avoid thinking that everything is over for Pride-and-joy (and there is no hint here of any life after death, where all manner of things might once more be well). If the story were to end with God's speech and the mark on Pride-and-joy's forehead, then we could go on further into the narrative with the straw still held tight in our hand. But it does not. There is another sentence:

So Pride-and-joy went out from before the face of the Lord, and settled in the land of Vagrancy, east of Eden. (4.16)

Out of its context the first part of this sentence could mean simply that he left the presence of God for the time being.

23

After what has gone before, it snatches away all hope. This elder brother and God will not, cannot, meet again. In the end there is no comfort. The tragedy is complete.

After this story there is a desperate need for a return to a theology of grace, and to a divine mercy which will create good out of evil. Once we reach Abraham and Sarah, that need will be met, and met over and over again. God's grace and his mercy beyond all deserving will become a major theme, perhaps *the* major theme of both the Old Testament and the New. But first things must get much worse. First there must be a Flood.

3

Only the Sound of Rain

(Genesis 6.6—9.17)

The Flood story is often regarded as a must for all children's Bibles, and the ark sometimes features on their covers. The dove that flies from the ark and returns with an olive branch in its beak has become a well-known and well-used symbol of peace, only outdone by the bright colours of the rainbow that appears at the story's end.

All this is rather surprising. For the Flood story is one of the darkest in all Scripture, and certain aspects of its theology are among the most disquieting we find anywhere. In my own preaching and storytelling, I have only been able to make room for it by speaking of the ark adrift on the ocean of God's tears. But that, I would at once acknowledge, is not how Genesis presents it. True, there is grief in heaven. True, this grief, caused by the violence and wickedness of humanity, supplies the reason for God's destruction of the earth (see Genesis 6.5–7). But beyond that Genesis refuses to go. God in Genesis regrets having created human beings (6.6, 7), but he does not regret destroying them. In a remarkable little passage near the end of the story (8.21–2), and again when he establishes a new covenant with the earth and all living things upon it, and sets the rainbow in the clouds as its sign (9.8–17), he vows never again to wreak such havoc, yet still he expresses no remorse.

The Flood in Genesis is a response to a humanity whose wickedness is complete (6.5), and which somehow has infected all the other creatures of the earth, so that the very earth is filthy and must be washed clean. At the end of the sixth day of creation in Genesis 1.29 we read, 'God looked at all he had made. See! Very good!' Now, at the start of the

Flood story, we find those words clearly echoed and then undone: 'God looked at the earth. See! Ruined!' (6.12) The extent of the tragedy could hardly be conveyed more power-fully, or succinctly. God at creation sees a paradise, where all is in place and as it should be, all is very beautiful, very good. Now, not six chapters later, he sees a vast Auschwitz stretching as far as his eye can see, and human beings consigning his bright earth to the gas chambers and the crematoria. His heart is broken. In the Garden, when he pronounced judgement upon the man and woman, and made clear to them what life outside Eden would be like, he spoke of a life of back-breaking toil and pain for each of them (Genesis 3.16 and 17[1]). Now the same pain has broken him also. When we read in 6.6 that 'he was *pained* in his heart', the Hebrew makes the echo of the Garden quite clear. God, it seems, is outside Eden himself now. For him, too, its lush delights are gone, with all its beauty, and all is ruined. His dreams lie shattered.

Yet let us be quite clear on this: the Flood is an utter cata-strophe, and entirely of God's doing. He plans it. He engineers it. By the terms of the story we are not dealing with a natural disaster on an unnatural scale. 'All the springs of the great deep erupted, and the floodgates of the skies were opened.' (7.11) That is how the coming of the Flood is described. We have not heard of 'the great deep' since the beginning of the Creation poem in Genesis 1, when 'the earth was topsy-turvy, and darkness lay upon the face of the deep' (1.2). In the minds of the ancient Israelites and their contemporaries in that part of the world, 'the deep' was a huge mass of water surrounding and underlying the land. God's second act of creation in Genesis 1 was to make a vault or dome to the sky, divide the deep into two, and put some of its waters above the dome. His third was to draw up boundaries for the waters left below the dome, thus letting dry land appear and making seas and lakes. Clearly, therefore, by opening the floodgates or windows in the dome here in Genesis 7, and by allowing the waters beneath the land to gush forth uncontrollably, God is returning his creation very nearly to square one. Only the unbroken succession of nights and days, and the creatures floating in the ark, distinguish the world of the Flood from the desolation of that first mass of water heaving in the dark. In Genesis 7, just six chapters after Creation, the Creator deliberately dismantles his creation.

Admittedly, there is a sense in which his actions only clarify the consequences of the wickedness of the earth. He brings ruin upon an earth which is already ruined.[2] We cannot save this God's skin, however, by saying the Flood was caused by the violence of his creatures and by leaving it at that. Nowadays, no doubt, we would write a story not of a flood, but of a nuclear holocaust, and Noah and his family and all the animals would build not an ark, but a concrete bunker. By the terms of Genesis we would have to have God pressing the buttons.

There is further reason for disquiet in the Genesis story. Claus Westermann, in his larger commentary, writes this:

> The actual description of the flood, which is really the main part, is relatively short. The reason for this brevity is that the coming and the effect of the flood are presented without comment or dialogue. There is no reaction from those involved; no lament, cry, death agony – nothing at all of this sort. There is absolute silence . . .[3]

In fact, there is no dialogue anywhere in the whole story, from its beginning in 6.5 to its end in 9.19. The only sound is the soft, persistent noise of the falling of the rain. There is much speech, certainly, but it is only found before the waters come and after they have disappeared, and all of it is put into the mouth of God. Noah and his family are silent throughout. God says a great deal to Noah before the Flood begins, and to him and his sons after it has abated, but not once do we hear them respond. Back on dry land Noah builds an altar and offers sacrifices upon it, and these attract God's attention, bring him close and soothe his heart. Yet this too is done in silence, without speech, without spoken prayer. Sacrifice is a form of prayer, of course, yet when we come to Noah's wordless ritual after the Garden of Eden and the field of Abel's death, where prayer was as natural as conversation, we sense at once the intimacy that has been lost. Communicating with God is not so simple as it was before, certainly in Eden. It is no longer as straightforward as speech, but involves the huge labour of altar-building and the complications of animal sacrifice. Religious ritual arises for Noah, as it does for us, out of the distance that human beings feel must lie between God and his creation. Sacrifice is inconceivable in the Garden of Eden. There is no need for religion till God is felt to be absent, and meeting him is problematic. That was so for Cain and Abel, or Pride-and-joy and Nobody, outside the Garden, at least at first. It is so after the Flood for Noah.

As for those who are drowned in the waters of the Flood, they are not even addressed. They are not warned. They are not given a chance to mend their ways. They cry no prayer of lament and complaint, or if they do, we do not hear it, nor is it spoken of. Even God himself has nothing to say while the destruction of the earth is proceeding. The waters wash away all life, except what is in the ark, and take speech along with it. It is the most terrible silence in all Scripture, and it is impossible to fill with any songs we might sing to God thanking him for saving those tucked up in the ark. Such songs sound hollow and quite out of place in the huge dark. In the end the Flood story offers more hope than we could have expected, but not because Noah and the rest are now safe back on dry land – the hope given there is limited. Hope arises because the Flood changes God.

> YHWH saw how great was the wickedness of human beings on earth, and that every plan, every thought of their hearts was thoroughly evil, and always so. YHWH was sorry he had made human beings on earth, and he was pained in his heart. YHWH said, 'I will wipe the human beings I have created from the face of the earth, human beings together with animals, reptiles, birds of the air, for I am sorry that I made them.' (6.5–7)

> The earth was ruined in God's eyes. The earth was full of violence. God looked at the earth. See! Ruined! All living things had ruined their ways upon the earth. God said to

Noah, 'It is the end of all living things. I have determined it. The earth is full of violence because of them. See, I am going to ruin them along with the earth.' (6.11–13)

So the Flood story begins. And this is how, when the waters have subsided and those in the ark are back on dry land, it approaches its conclusion:

Noah built an altar to YHWH, took of every clean animal and every clean bird and offered them as offerings upon the altar. When YHWH smelled the soothing smell, YHWH said in his heart, 'Never again will I curse the earth on account of human beings, though any plan of the human heart is evil from youth onwards. Never again will I strike down all that lives as I have done.

> All the days the earth remains,
> sowing and harvest,
> cold and heat,
> summer and winter,
> day and night
> shall not cease.'

And God blessed Noah and his sons, and said to them, 'Be fruitful and multiply, and fill the earth.' (8.20—9.1)

There is a teasing ambiguity at a crucial point in the last passage. Is it, in Genesis 8.21, 'Never again will I curse the earth on account of human beings, *though* any plan of the human heart is evil from youth onwards,' as I have translated it, or, '*because* any plan of the human heart is evil from youth onwards,' or again, 'because any plan of the human heart *was* evil from youth onwards'? The Hebrew text includes no 'is' nor 'was', but leaves the matter open, and though our English versions invariably settle for the former, the latter remains an option. As for the way the clause begins, the Hebrew word involved, *ki*, is a very common one, but the most common words are sometimes the hardest to translate, for they can bear the largest range of meanings. Undoubtedly *ki* is much more common in the sense of 'because' than 'though', yet there are a significant number of verses in the Old Testament where the second meaning is agreed.[4] The trouble with Genesis 8.21 is that the context does very little to remove the uncertainties. 'Though' makes obvious sense, but on the other hand God could simply be rehearsing the reason why he brought the Flood in the first place, and such a meaning would clearly be conveyed if we were to opt for *'was* evil from youth onwards'.

Whichever translation we choose, however, three things are, or soon become, plain: the storyteller is deliberately echoing the language he used at the start of the Flood story; he has moderated the terms of that earlier passage; and, as far as human nature is concerned, nothing has changed.

'Every plan, every thought of their hearts was thoroughly evil, and always so', (6.5) is now repeated in the form, 'any plan of the human heart is/was evil from youth onwards' (8.21). Anger has turned to resignation. The fearful passion of the first statement has been spent in the havoc of the Flood. Its emphatic, staccato language, so striking in the Hebrew, has now been softened, soothed by the sweet aroma of the sacrifice.

Yet human beings have not changed. That is not immediately clear in the story, unless we persist in translating 8.21 as, 'though any plan of the human heart is evil from youth onwards'. If instead we translate, *'because* any plan of the human heart *was* evil from youth onwards', then God could simply be looking back to the humanity destroyed in the Flood. In that case we have to wait and see how Noah and his sons fare, and their descendants after them.

We do not have to wait long. We do not even have to wait till the Flood story is over. The ancient blessing of creation, repeated after Noah's sacrifice, 'Be fruitful and multiply, and fill the earth' (9.1; see 1.28) is followed by God's declaring,

'Fear of you, dread of you shall be upon all the animals of the earth, all the birds of the skies, all that creeps on the ground, all the fish of the sea. Into your hand they are given. Every moving thing that lives will be food for you;

just as I gave you the green plants, so I give you everything.'
(9.2–3)

A new note is struck here. Back in Genesis 1 God gave the
newly created human beings royal, almost divine status, and
granted them the sovereignty of the earth and all its creatures.
But there was no talk then of 'fear' or 'dread'. There was no
hint of war between human beings and the other creatures
of the earth, such as the words 'fear' and 'dread' convey. The
sovereignty to be exercised by human beings was to be an
entirely benign one, characterized by the vegetarian diet
which they were to follow. There was to be no killing for
food. There was to be no killing. Instead they were to keep
the new earth in the good and beautiful order in which God
had made it. At that point the God of Genesis did not know
what human beings were like. Now, after the Flood, he
knows only too well. He has seen how they exercise their
power. He has seen them consume his creation with their
violence. All he can do is try to limit their slaughter, by outlaw-
ing the killing of other human beings, and by forbidding the
consumption of any animal's life-blood (9.4–6).

All this is in anticipation of what will ensue, but the next
episode returns us to actuality. Noah gets drunk and is found
and terribly disgraced by one of his sons. The result of that is
the pronouncement of a curse and the breaking apart of the
family that has survived the Flood (9.20–7). As if that were
not disappointment enough, the next story, following after a
genealogy giving us the descendants of Noah's sons, is that of
the Tower of Babel. There human beings attempt to ignore
the divine command to 'fill the earth' by congregating in one
place, and that leads to the disintegration of this larger human
family, and further damage to the relationship between its
members and their God. It is the same old story, and will
remain so till the great narrative of Genesis—Kings is done.

The Flood has not changed human beings, but it has
changed God. Genesis 1 presented God in majestic control of
events, able without struggle, without conflict, without any
apparent effort, to create the world. Near the end of the

Creation poem he gave acres of that power away to the human beings he had made. In the Flood story he takes that power back into his own hands. For the last time. At the end he vows never to destroy his creation again, and sets the rainbow in the sky to remind him. The promise is far more than an assurance that he will never again unleash the forces of chaos. It amounts to a pledge that he will never again seek absolute control of events. He will retain the status, the dignity, the freedom for human beings he first gave them at Creation. He will allow them their power, however they choose to exercise it, and whatever the cost for the rest of his creation. He will live with them, whatever the price he has to pay. (Little did the storyteller know that it would one day cost him death on a cross, or that the power to destroy the earth, which God after the Flood surrenders, would one day be gained by human beings themselves through their invention of the nuclear bomb, or through other technological and industrial developments so threatening of the earth's delicate balance.)

After the Flood, we enter a new era in the generosity, the patience and the pain of the God of Genesis, and find all the creatures of the earth, including human beings, granted a new security. The rhythms of the earth can now be relied upon. No threat of destruction hangs over them. Human violence will no longer meet with the punishment it deserves. Ruin will not be answered with ruin. The demands of mercy can, inevitably will, transcend those of justice. The world after the Flood has more room for God's grace. Grace is built into the new order of things.

Here lies the true hope of this story. Most of its readers place it elsewhere, in the favour Noah finds in the sight of God, and the rescue of him and his family and their cargo of animals. Noah, however, is not typical. Near its start (6.9) the story describes him as 'a just man', and, admittedly, there are plenty of 'just' people in the Old Testament. But it then calls him 'blameless', and there are far fewer of those. Finally it says he 'walked with God', and of only one other person, Enoch in Genesis 5.22, 24, is that said. Though the story of his drunkenness will bring him down to earth with a bump, Noah's

32

goodness is of a very rare order, extremely unusual in any age, and unique in his own. We are not Noahs, most of us. If the safety of the ark is only for the most saintly of saints, then we are lost. There is not much comfort for us to draw from the ark. The comfort of the Flood story lies in the promises God makes when the waters have gone, promises whose circles spread so wide that they embrace not only all humanity, but all living things, and the earth itself on which they depend.

Yet if the story ends with such hope and room for grace, does this mean a return to the old intimacies of the Garden? There are two incidental details of the Flood story, which might suggest it does. One we have noticed already, and that is God's 'smelling' the smell of Noah's sacrifice. The other comes earlier, when Noah and the others are safely inside the ark. God 'shuts' them in (7.16). For all we said earlier about the significance of sacrifice, such bold talk as this of God's 'smelling' and 'shutting' is the language of Eden. We have not heard it since then, and indeed we will not hear it again in the Bible. People will tell us the language used of God after this will become more sophisticated. We might say it will speak less directly of God's intimacy.

Yet what does this intimacy amount to here? Two incidental details are not much. Admittedly, with their great rarity they cannot be insignificant. They belong only to Genesis, and even in Genesis only to its very early chapters. They make their own contribution to the poignancy of these chapters, for they give us the sense that in their passing they take with them an intimacy with God which is no more, the intimacy by which and for which we were made. Nevertheless, they remain but faint traces of the world of the Garden. For us to have re-entered Eden through the Flood story, we would have needed far more speech from Noah at least, if not from his wife and the other members of his family; we would have needed dialogue, and far more colour in Noah's cheeks. Instead, as we have emphasized already, there is no dialogue at all. The first words and the last Noah ever speaks are not even found in the Flood story, but are those he uses in the following episode to curse Canaan (9.25–7). Throughout the

Flood story he remains a shadowy figure. It seems the story-teller deliberately avoids giving us any glimpse of his hero's feelings.[5] We learn nothing of any fear of Noah's, nothing of any grief, and are left to guess at any relief and gratitude he feels once the disaster is over from the altar he builds and the sacrifices he offers upon it. We might be tempted to say he acts like a robot, a kind of compliant automaton, but in truth the story does not tell us enough about him for us even to think that. He does not emerge as a human being of flesh and blood recognizably like ours until he gets drunk and goes to sleep, indecently dishevelled in his tent!

This dark story of the Flood leaves us with many things. One of them, undoubtedly, is a longing for a return to some speaking on the part of human beings, some plain-speaking, some addressing of God, some prayer, some dialogue. In Genesis we have to wait a short while, but then we come to Abraham.

4

Telling God how to be God

(Genesis 18.16–33)

What, in Genesis, is Abraham's finest hour? Many, brought up with the plaudits of the New Testament ringing in their ears, and regarding Abraham as the archetypal person of faith, might say he had not one but two finest hours: his obeying the command to leave for a new land of God's choosing (Genesis 12.1–5), and his equally obedient taking of his son Isaac to the brink of sacrifice (Genesis 22). Such wordless obedience has often been presented in the Christian Church as a model for the way human beings should respond to God, and still is so. 'If only we could have such faith and trust in God as Abraham! If only we could show such selflessness, such a willingness to part with what is dear to us for the sake of God and his larger purposes!' That has been, still is, I dare say, the burden of many a sermon on him.

Yet we may find Abraham's obedience in those two episodes unnerving. In the first he does not speak at all, while in the second his only words to God are 'Here I am', spoken at the start, before God issues the command, and again when he has the knife poised at his son's throat. In the Hebrew 'Here I am' is just one word. His general silence reminds us of the silence of Noah in the Flood story, and ironically, in the story of the binding of Isaac, it also calls to our minds the initial silence of Cain or Pride-and-joy.

In Genesis 12 there is no prayer, no dialogue with God at all, no protest. The commands from God to leave his country, his past, his roots, his culture, his sense of belonging, his status and position in society and the family, his friendships, the love of those close to him, all those in his family except for his wife and his nephew, are received by Abraham in silence and obeyed in silence. 'So Abram went, as YHWH had spoken to him ... and he took his wife Sarai and his nephew Lot, all the possessions they possessed and the persons they had acquired in Haran, and they set out for the land of Canaan.' (Genesis 12.4, 5) That is all. Sarai and Lot seem to have no say in the matter, let alone their slaves. Speaking more literally, Abraham has no say in the matter either. He says nothing.

His silence is much more strange, much more alarming in Genesis 22. 'Take your son, your one and only that you love, Isaac, go to the land of Moriah, and offer him up there as an offering upon one of the mountains that I will tell you about.' (22.2) It is a terrifying command and utterly bewildering. From the beginning Abraham's stories in Genesis have been overshadowed by the seemingly impossible promise from God of a son. At last, quite beyond the expectations of Abraham and Sarah, that son has been born. Now God commands Abraham to sacrifice him. It makes no apparent sense whatever. It seems capricious and intolerably cruel. So how might we reasonably expect Abraham to react? What might the Old Testament itself lead us to think he will say, when its prayer so often exhibits such marvellously plain speaking? Might we not anticipate a cry of anguish sharp enough to split the heavens, and howls of protest meant to shrink God's heart? Might we not think that Abraham will demand from God, at the very least, an explanation? What, in fact, we hear is this: 'So Abraham got up early in the morning, saddled his ass, took two of his young men with him and Isaac his son, split the wood for the offering, arose and went to the place which God told him about.' (22.3)

It is astonishing, but what is even more disconcerting is that often we fail to be astonished. Indeed, many of us have been carefully taught to be full of admiration, prompted, it is true, by the end of the story itself, where God commends Abraham in such fulsome speech for his obedience (22.15–18). Worse still, with Abraham's example before us, we have been encouraged to think that such ready submission to the will of God is what is required of us, and that it is not ours to question or protest, even if his demands seem intolerable. That way, we are told, lies saintliness. In truth that particular road forks either towards a religion that keeps us as children in the presence of God and prevents us from growing up, or else towards an unquestioning and unhesitating fanaticism.

Though the Bible, in both its Testaments, has much to say about the sovereignty of God, and the need for human obedience, it contains another strain we have referred to in several places, and indeed already begun to encounter in the story of the Garden and in the story of Pride-and-joy and Nobody. There we find no silent subservience, no self-surrender or eager prostration, but robust challenge, a bid for partnership with God, or an assumption of it, not a burying of the face before his feet, but a looking him in the eye.

But we do not need to go back to the very earliest chapters of Genesis to find it, or beyond the stories of Abraham and Sarah. One of its most remarkable expressions in all Scripture occurs within those stories, in the second half of Genesis 18. The first part of the chapter does little to prepare us for what is to come. There Abraham finds God standing near the entrance to his tent in the heat of the day, washes his feet (or gets his slave to do it for him – the storyteller does not bother with that detail), and entertains him to a gigantic meal (18.1–15). Yet in one sense Abraham does not find God there, for God comes in disguise, and though he starts flinging about all sorts of hints about his true identity, it seems as though Abraham fails to catch any of them. Sarah, too, remains in the dark, and not just in the literal gloom of the tent, unless her fear at the end contains a sudden sense of awe.[1] The extraordinary image of God sitting down to Abraham's and Sarah's cakes and roast beef might seem to take us right back into the heart of Eden, and return us to its natural intimacies. But God's disguise creates a distance which was not there in Eden. The story contains dialogue aplenty, but no prayer, for Abraham does not know who he is speaking to, and we cannot be sure that Sarah, who only has two words in the Hebrew to say to God in any case, understands either. The intimacy between God and Abraham in the next passage, in 18.16–33, is far greater, even if there is no mention of footwashing or the eating of beef. Then Abraham will know exactly who he is speaking to, and if he was obtuse before, now he will have such wisdom that he can teach God how to be God. *This*, surely, will be his finest hour.

> The men rose from there, and looked down on Sodom laid out before them. Abraham went with them to set them on their way. (18.16)

That is how it begins. For the moment we are still in the world of the previous tale. God is still disguised as a man, as is each of his two companions. Abraham is still preoccupied with the demands of hospitality, concerned to set his guests upon the right road and to accompany them along it for a spell. But now there occurs a radical shift. God throws aside his disguise, to allow us, the hearers or readers of the story, to enter the secrets of his thoughts. As for Abraham, when he next appears, he will hardly be recognizable as the same man, and will turn his mind, and God's mind too, to much weightier matters than cakes and beef and the road to the local town.

> YHWH said, 'Am I going to conceal from Abraham what I am about to do, when Abraham shall become, yes become a great and powerful nation, and all the nations of the earth will be blessed through him? For I have singled him out, so he might charge his children and his household after him to keep the way of YHWH by doing what is just and right, so that YHWH might bring about for him what he has promised for him.' Then YHWH said, 'The outcry against Sodom and Gomorrah, how great it is! Their sin, how very oppressive! Let me go down and see whether their deeds quite match the outcry that has reached me: if not, I will know.' (18.17–21)
> Then the men turned from there, and went towards Sodom and Gomorrah, while YHWH still stood before Abraham. Abraham came near and said, 'Will you really sweep away the innocent along with the guilty? What if there are fifty innocent people somewhere in the city? Will you really sweep them away? Will you not forgive the place

because of the fifty innocent people inside it? Profanation! You do such a thing? Put to death the innocent with the guilty! The same for the innocent and the guilty! Profanation! How could you? Will not the judge of the whole earth do what is just?' (18.22–5)

YHWH said, 'If I find fifty innocent people somewhere in the city of Sodom, I will forgive the whole place because of them.'

Abraham answered, 'Look, please, I have taken it upon myself to speak to my lord, and me just dust and ashes. What if of the fifty innocent people, five are missing? Because of the missing five will you destroy the whole city?'

He said, 'I will not destroy it, if I find forty five there.' (18.26–8)

Again he spoke to him and said, 'What if forty people are found there?'

He said, 'For the sake of forty I will not do it.'

He said, 'Please do not be angry, my lord, if I speak further. What if thirty are found there?'

He said, 'I will not do it, if I find thirty there.'

He said, 'Look, please, I have taken it upon myself to speak to my lord. What if twenty are found there?'

He said, 'For the sake of twenty I will not destroy it.'

He said, 'Please do not be angry, my lord, if I speak this once more. What if ten are found there?'

He said, 'For the sake of ten I will not destroy it.'

Then YHWH went on his way, having finished speaking with Abraham, and Abraham went home. (18.29–33)

It is easy to get carried away when talking about this dialogue. Let us be cautious in what we say: it is certainly *one* of the most remarkable in the entire Bible! Some of Moses' encounters with God will come very close to this, and Job, in his speeches to or about God will match and more than match Abraham's plain speaking. But even they will not tell God quite so directly how to be God. Even they will not produce a speech quite like Abraham's first one here, in 18.23–5.

This is not the first time Abraham has engaged in dialogue

with God. The promises he receives in 12.1–3 and again in chapter 13.14–17 speak of offspring, and in 15.2–3 he voices his frustration and bewilderment at his failing to have a child in no uncertain terms: 'My lord YHWH, what are you going to give me, when I am going to die childless . . . ? Look, you have given me no offspring, and see now, a member of my household is going to be my heir!'

Five verses later he asks a straight question about the land promised to him: 'My lord YHWH, how can I know I am going to take possession of it?' (15.8)

This is the point at which Abraham's relationship with God achieves some maturity. No longer is he like a child simply being told by the parent what to do, or being given promises of gifts to be accepted, apparently, without question. Now he approaches God as an adult, prepared to show him how he feels, and to question, challenge and accuse. After each speech he receives immediate reassurance.

But the portrayal of Abraham in the Genesis cycle of stories about him is not consistent. When we reach God's establishing his covenant with him in chapter 17, where God has considerably more to say to him than anywhere else, we find, perhaps to our surprise, hardly any dialogue at all. Abraham does challenge the promise of a child to him and Sarah: 'Can a child be born to someone who is a hundred, and can Sarah bear a child when she is ninety?' (17.17) But he only thinks these words, or says them to himself. Indeed, at this point there is a breakdown in communication. For Abraham is prostrate before God, in the attitude of worship and submission, yet is laughing at the promise and its seeming impossibility. His laughter is prophetic, for in the Hebrew 'he laughed' is precisely the same as the name Isaac which the promised child will be given. Yet it remains the laughter of mockery. Abraham is not looking God in the eye here. There is no honest prayer. Instead he sniggers at God's feet. True, he goes on to face God with, 'If only Ishmael could live in your sight!' (17.18) Just four words in the Hebrew, they are the only ones he addresses to God in the whole chapter. They put forward an alternative to God's declared plan, suggesting that

Ishmael, who is Abraham's son, though not Sarah's, and who has the advantage of already having been born, might inherit instead. But the words seek to conceal the mockery, the disbelief, the pain and sense of loss of the thoughts or words entertained in the laughter. That is still the case, though God at once sees through the pretence.

Thus, by the time we reach the dialogue in 18.23–33, only 15.2–3, and to a lesser degree 15.8, have in any way prepared us for what we find.

If we have read our way through Genesis, we have heard of Sodom and Gomorrah before, and of the wickedness of Sodom and of its coming destruction, together with Gomorrah's, at the hands of God (see Genesis 13.10, 13). Genesis 19 will take us down into the heart of Sodom and allow us to witness its terror for ourselves. Unfortunately, the city has lent its name and its condemnation to homosexual practices, but only as a result of a shallow reading of the Genesis text.[2] What is actually described in the horrifying confrontation between Lot and the men of Sodom in 19.4–11 is threatened gang rape and likely murder, racism, and an utter disregard for the demands of hospitality, for the particular needs of immigrants, and for male honour and dignity.[3]

Abraham in his dialogue with God in 18.23–33 nowhere denies that Sodom is a wicked place, nor does he question God's right to punish or destroy evil. On the contrary, as 'judge of the whole earth' God *must* confront evil. But, says Abraham, he must not pursue the guilty at the expense of the innocent. Significantly, he initiates the dialogue, and, even more important, dares to take on the role of God's teacher.

God's words or thoughts of 18.17–21 are not addressed to Abraham, but to himself, or to the members of his heavenly court. They are for our benefit, the readers or hearers of the story. They purport to give us an insight into the mind of God, and reveal the plans up his sleeve. Sometimes, as in the case of Job, in Job 1—2, such insight is ours alone and is denied to the other protagonists in the drama. In this case Abraham seems to have overheard, for his opening speech sounds like a response to what God has just said. Such over-hearing puts him at once in a highly privileged position, inside God's inner circle, and indeed God himself has already spoken of him in such terms. He has already told us he has chosen to divulge his plan to investigate Sodom and Gomorrah to Abraham, because he is the bearer of the promises. We are reminded of his warning Noah, and only Noah, about the Flood.

It might seem curious that God does not choose to tell Abraham of the threat to Sodom and Gomorrah because their territories are part of the promised land, or because Lot, his nephew, has taken up residence in Sodom with his family (see Genesis 13.8–12). Beyond the promise that he will become the ancestor of a great and powerful nation, God only refers in his first speech to Abraham's becoming a source of blessing to the other nations of the earth, and his call to be an exemplar of what is just and right. But Abraham seems to have overheard that too, for he does not refer in his dialogue to Lot and the promised land either, but says a great deal about what is just and right, and seeks to shift God's preoccupation in a direction that will, if heeded, almost inevitably result in blessing for other nations, even a place like Sodom.

Yet the privileges that Abraham enjoys would still not seem to have put him in the position of God's teacher. God may have singled him out to teach his children and his household what is just and right, but he has not appointed him as his own tutor in such matters! Yet that is the role Abraham adopts in this passage. Both he and also those who transmitted the Hebrew text of the passage acknowledge his remarkable audacity. Most translations of 18.22 have something like this: 'So the men turned from there, and went towards Sodom, while Abraham remained standing before the Lord.' (NRSV) That is a true reflection of the Hebrew text that has come down to us from the rabbis and scribes of the early centuries of the Common Era. If you open a Hebrew Bible, that is what you will find. But textual critics tell us that what the text had originally was, 'while *YHWH* still stood before *Abraham*', and that this was changed because of the demands of Jewish piety. To 'stand before someone' in the Old Testament can mean to act as their slave, and the handlers of the text did not want to leave the impression that God's status was beneath Abraham's.[4]

Abraham himself quickly becomes aware of his daring. 'Look, please, I have taken it upon myself to speak to my lord, and me just dust and ashes.' We can almost hear his knees beginning to knock. The first part of that speech he repeats later, and twice he begs God not to be angry.

Yet God is not angry. Even after that first speech, he does not flinch, let alone fly into a rage. Instead he at once accepts Abraham's terms, and goes on accepting them to the very end. Plain speaking, even such audacious, seemingly presumptuous plain speaking as Abraham's here, is never condemned in the Old Testament, despite a handful of passages which, in particular circumstances, challenge the questioning of God.[5]

God's ready and continued acceptance of Abraham's terms indicates at once that the dialogue is not a piece of bartering, as some have supposed. If it were that, then it would run something like this: 'What if there are fifty innocent people in the city ...?' 'Fifty! *Fifty!* You must be joking! Five hundred.' 'Don't be ridiculous! Seventy five.' 'Four hundred and fifty.' And so on, ending up somewhere around three hundred. This dialogue between Abraham and God does not take place in the *suq*, but in the court room, or the theology lecture room. And Abraham has God in the dock, or sitting at a desk beneath his dais!

Abraham, again appearing to have overheard God's initial speech or read his thoughts, starts with God's determination to destroy Sodom. That might seem to go beyond God's plan to go down to Sodom to see what the inhabitants are really like. But he has already declared their sin very oppressive, and when, before that, he wonders about telling Abraham what he is going to do, it is as if he has already made up his mind. Abraham seems to have picked that up, as well as the nature of God's preoccupation. For what is God 'going down' to Sodom to see? What kind of people is he expecting to find, and what kind of people is he going there to look for? The answer is contained in his words that immediately precede the dialogue: 'Let me go down and see whether their deeds quite match the outcry that has reached me: if not, I will know.' (18.21) God is preoccupied with sin and guilt, with searching out the guilty. His ears are filled with the outcry *against* Sodom.[6] Abraham tries to shift his focus, and encourages him to listen for another, fainter sound. 'When you go down to Sodom,' he tells God, 'don't look for the wicked, look for the good people, the just and the righteous people. And if you find them, spare the whole city, so that they do not get caught up in a punishment they do not deserve. If you find just a tiny handful [Abraham *starts* with only fifty!], then let *them* determine the fate of the place. Don't be preoccupied with punishing the guilty, for if you are, innocent people are bound to suffer. Listen for the outcry of the innocent, and be concerned with giving them their just deserts, and be so preoccupied and single-minded about that, that you forgive the whole community and allow the guilty to go unpunished. You vowed after the Flood to live with a violent and wicked humanity, whatever it cost you. Remember that! Look at the rainbow! It is different now. You have a world now which Noah can save from destruction, merely through his goodness!'

That, in effect, is what Abraham says and persists in saying in this passage. It is remarkable enough, of course. Cries for justice to be done in our own society, and in the Bible also, seem more often concerned with the guilty being duly punished. A world in which a tiny handful of good people can ensure that wickedness goes unpunished might seem frighteningly chaotic, and, indeed, a flagrant denial of justice. Abraham persists, however. If punishing the guilty means innocent people suffering, then better not punish at all; better forgive and take the consequences.

His stance is positively shocking when we recall the place he is talking about. He is talking about the possibility of the violent people of *Sodom* being let off the hook. The extent of their violence will soon be made plain in the episode of the near gang rape in Genesis 19. And there are plenty of other passages in the Old Testament to show how notorious a city it was in the tradition.

Abraham is trying to teach God what exercising justice means, what being 'the judge of the whole earth' entails. No-one else in Scripture tries to do that, not so overtly, at least. No-one else asks, 'Will not the judge of the whole earth do justice?' Yet Abraham goes beyond even this. He tells God that if he does not heed what he says, if he goes ahead and destroys the innocent along with the guilty, then God will effectively cease to be God. For his actions will be profane, defiled, polluted, a desecration.[7] No longer will he be holy, and not to be holy is not to be God. That is why we can describe Abraham in this passage as not merely teaching God how to do justice, but instructing him how to be God.

And he succeeds! Or so it seems at first. God accepts his teaching without hesitation once, twice ... six times. 'If I find fifty innocent people somewhere in the city of Sodom, I will forgive the whole place because of them ... For the sake of forty I will not do it ... For the sake of ten I will not destroy it.' And when the two divine companions of God go down to Sodom that evening, they make a bee-line for Lot and his family! (19.1–3) They go straight for an innocent family! Sodom will surely be saved now, and Lot and his family will have secured its salvation!

The whole episode ends, however, with Abraham getting up the following morning, going to the spot where he had taught God his lesson, looking down on Sodom and Gomorrah ... and seeing the smoke and flames of their burning (19.27–8). Lot has not saved Sodom, nor its neighbour Gomorrah, after all. True, he and his family are safe, except for his wife, who in the end could not quite bring herself to leave the city behind. They are safe, however, not because Abraham's teaching has been acted upon, but because God's companions have got them out of harm's way in the nick of time. They made straight for Lot's house, not because they were determined to search out the innocent, but because they knew they would have to rescue him and his family from the coming destruction. When they urged him to get the family together and escape from the city, they explained with the words, 'We are about to destroy this place, for such an outcry against it has reached YHWH, and YHWH has sent us to destroy it.' (19.13) Their speech clearly echoes the words of God that came before the dialogue with Abraham (see 18.20–1). Though in the dialogue of 18.23–32 God agreed with Abraham at every turn, it is now as if it had never happened. If God were to find a handful of innocent people in Sodom, Abraham was not asking him to engineer their escape so he could get on with the job of destroying the rest. He was asking him to leave them there, and spare the whole community. He was asking for an exercise of justice that makes generous room for mercy and grace, even for effective vicarious suffering – for in a violent, lawless place like Sodom any innocent people who might ensure its survival will hardly be able to expect an easy time of it. God seemed then to understand. He seemed to agree. He was surely speaking to him, to use a description of Moses from the book of Exodus, 'face to face, as one speaks to a friend' (Exodus 33.11).[8] Abraham himself was most certainly looking him in the eye. Surely God was returning his gaze? *Together*, surely, they arrived at an understanding of what doing justice, being God, meant. The prayer of the dialogue seemed to create a new maturity in their relationship, a true partnership.

We are not told what Abraham thinks and feels as he looks down from his high ridge upon the fierce conflagration beneath him, and sees what was once like the Garden of Eden (see Genesis 13.10) becoming the desolation of the borders of the Dead Sea. The storyteller leaves that to our imagination, and inevitably so, for how could he describe Abraham's reaction to watching his vision of justice, his friendship with God, his understanding of God and his holiness, and all hope of grace for the world, going up in the smoke of Sodom and Gomorrah?

Sometimes in the Bible the storytelling is so powerful, so disconcerting in its theology, so uncomfortable in its challenge, that the narrative or the poetry will immediately draw back into safer territory, where things are more conventional and predictable. For example, the astonishing vision in Isaiah 53 of the Servant of God effecting the salvation of the many through his own agony is never repeated, not until Golgotha, at least. So here in Genesis we descend from the heights of Abraham's astounding vision to the plain of a more predictable world, and a more predictable God, a God and a world much more comforting for those who consider themselves among the innocent, where the wicked get what they deserve. From the position of our own faith we might try to comfort Abraham by telling him God *could* absorb, *did* absorb his teaching, only the narrator, or the compiler of the Genesis narrative could not.

His failure is not surprising. *Our* failure is disastrous.

5

Naming the Unnameable[1]

(Genesis 16.7–16; 21.8–21)

In March 1996 a party of us from Chester Cathedral went on pilgrimage to Israel/Palestine. We stayed in an Arab hotel in East Jerusalem, and one Sunday evening at our invitation Cedar Duaybis came to speak to us. Cedar is a Palestinian Christian, who has spent most of her life in Nablus and Ramallah, and who is a member of the Executive Committee of Sabeel, the Liberation Theology Centre in Jerusalem. Sometimes we find an occasion especially memorable because truth is told as we have not heard it told before, and because a humanity is revealed so striking that we are reminded once more what it means to be human. I will not forget that meeting with Cedar Duaybis. She described the terrible suffering of the Palestinian people, and their loneliness in the international community. 'No-one needs Palestinians,' she said. 'We are seen as troublemakers wherever we go.' She told us of the difficulties faced by Palestinian Christians, a tiny minority of the population and shrinking. She explained that Palestinian women had been in the forefront of the *Intifada*, guarding their homes, keeping their families together, but without their part being sufficiently recognized. She spoke also of the problems she herself had encountered as a woman, outside the safe confines of Sabeel. 'No-one listens to women,' she said. 'I am a Palestinian, Christian, woman . . . three times oppressed.'

Hagar, the subject of our study in this chapter, is an Egyptian, slave, woman . . . three times oppressed.

Hagar becomes many things to many people. Most especially, all sorts of rejected women find their stories in her. She is the faithful maid exploited, the black woman used by the male and abused by the female of the ruling class,

the surrogate mother, the resident alien without legal
recourse, the other woman, the runaway youth, the religious
fleeing from affliction [or, we might add, the person trying
to escape tyrannical religion], the pregnant young woman
alone, the expelled wife, the divorced mother with child,
the shopping bag lady carrying bread and water, the
homeless woman, the indigent relying on handouts from
the power structures, the welfare mother, and the self-
effacing female whose own identity shrinks in service to
others.

So writes the American scholar, Phyllis Trible.[2]

Hagar, three times oppressed. Four times, if Savina Teubal
is to be believed.[3] Behind the Genesis stories of Hagar in the
desert Teubal detects the figure of a 'Desert Matriarch',
clothed in the language of a goddess, mother of a semi-
divine child, ancestress of the Hagarite people (to which we
find reference in 1 Chronicles 5.10, 19–20; 27.30 and Psalm
83.6) and commemorated at seasonal festivals at her shrine at
Beer-lahai-roi. Those who passed on the traditions effectively
demoted her, so Teubal argues, to slave and concubine,
removed any mention of the people who bore her name,
made Abraham the father of her child, and gave him such
prominence that her role as matriarch and ancestress is almost
obliterated.

Yet even as they have come down to us, the Genesis Hagar
stories are very far from being simply stories of oppression.
Hagar, in the two stories we will examine, is not merely
victim of other people's cruelty or contempt. The first begins
with her taking the initiative, and the second ends with her
doing so again. Her second initiative is of a kind that deter-
mines the course of history, while the first leads to an encounter
with God, which holds several large surprises and is unique in
several respects.

For a start the story of that first encounter contains the most
substantial dialogue between God and a woman to be found
in Scripture. The only other examples are the one with the
woman in the Garden of Eden, and the tiny dialogue with

Sarah in Genesis 18.15, which amounts to, ' "I did not laugh." "No, but you did laugh." ' (I have already remarked in an earlier chapter upon the Bible's neglect of the spiritual life of women.[4]) God in Genesis 16.6–16, and again in 21.9–21, pays Hagar an attention which is rare indeed, and which puts her in the company of a Mary of Nazareth entertaining heaven, or a Mary of Magdala, distraught beside a garden tomb on the morning of Resurrection. We shall find, indeed, that this Hagar is a visionary, whose eyes are opened to new truths, and whose plight and whose response remind us of what is essential to our being human.

Hagar's first story begins with Sarai, Abram's wife (they do not become Sarah and Abraham till Genesis 17). Hagar is Sarai's slave-woman, acquired, we must presume, when she and Abram were in Egypt (see Genesis 12.10–20). Sarai is, or seems, unable to have children. That is the first thing we are told about her, when she appears in the narrative (11.30). That is what the narrator wishes us to remember about her, as his God gives fine promises to Abram, and later assures him he will have a son so that they can begin to find some fulfilment. How can Abram have a son, when it seems Sarai is unable to conceive, and he has no other wife? That is the problem set by the storyteller, and his stories of Abram and Sarai, or Abraham and Sarah as they become, are largely concerned with its resolution.

Sarai is the first to propose a solution, though, as far as we know, she has not heard God's promises for herself, and may not realize the significance of her plan.[5] She offers her slave-woman, Hagar, as a second wife to Abram, in the hope that she will bear him a child. Hagar will remain Sarai's slave, and any child will be handed over to her mistress, and be counted as hers. Hagar, in other words, is to become a surrogate mother for Sarai's and Abram's benefit. Her own wishes and feelings, of course, do not come into the matter. She is, after all, only a slave, and a foreign one at that.

Hagar has no trouble conceiving (and the child will, of course, turn out to be a son!), but Sarai has a great deal of trouble dealing with the consequences. '. . . when she [Hagar] saw that she had conceived, her mistress became contemptible in her eyes.' (16.4) This is too much for Sarai. She has borne too much humiliation already, not just as a result of year after year passing by without her having a child, but because of the cruelty of her husband.[6] Whether Hagar's contempt is real or imagined by Sarai, we cannot tell. But for Sarai it is the last straw. She had looked forward to having a child, but she knows the child will never be hers. Whatever the customs of her society, the child will always be Hagar's. Hagar will see to that. Sarai knows that now. She had looked forward to a new status, to being able at last to hold her head high. Instead she has found yet further degradation.

In desperation and in anger she appeals to Abram. He simply reminds her that Hagar is her slave, and that she can do with her whatever she likes (16.6). His cold words, so devoid of any feeling for the wife who bears his child, and of any real sympathy for the one who cannot, give Sarai permission to turn her anger in Hagar's direction. That is at once what she does. Having taken it out on her husband, she now takes it out on her slave. She abuses her power over her. She abuses her. Her regime becomes tyrannical, as terrible as the one her descendants and Abram's will one day have to endure in Egypt (God's prediction of that period in Egypt to Abram, so recently made in 15.13, contains the same Hebrew verb to describe the oppression). Sarai's and Abram's descendants will have to escape from tyranny in order to survive. Hagar decides she must do the same. For the first time in her story she seizes the initiative. She runs away, taking with her in her womb the child Abram has given her.

The Israelites will only escape from Egypt with the help of Moses and Aaron, and the terrifying acts of God. Hagar, trying to escape *to* Egypt, as yet has no-one on her side. She simply runs away, and heads for home. Her route takes her through the Negev. It is a long way to the Egyptian border, but she is getting close to it, when God stops her in her tracks.

The messenger of YHWH found her by the spring of water in the desert, by the spring on the way to Shur. He said,

'Hagar, Sarai's slave-woman. Where have you come from? Where are you going?'

She replied, 'Me? I am running away from my mistress, Sarai.'

The messenger of YHWH said to her, 'Go back to your mistress, and submit yourself to her abuse.' (16.7–9)

The meeting takes place at a spot that was obviously well known to the first hearers of the story. Most English translations call it 'a spring of water'. But the Hebrew is more naturally translated '*the* spring', and there is no need to change that. At the end of the story we will be given its name, Beer-lahai-roi. It is not just any spring. It is *the* spring that marks the spot of Hagar's encounter. Israel/Palestine is full of such holy sites. Millions go to see them every year, to recall particular moments when, so they believe, God was seen and heard with rare clarity, and to make those moments their own. No doubt, in the days when this story was first told, Hagar's spring was such a site, a place where she was remembered (worshipped originally, if Savina Teubal is correct), and where many came to find the Truth as she had done.

But who is this 'messenger of God'? We have not heard of such a figure before in Genesis. Some translations speak of an 'angel', but that puts into our minds notions which were only developed long after Genesis was written. For the moment we must preserve the mystery of the language. We will soon have an inkling of an answer, and we will know it by the end. But we can notice what the description does. Not only does it keep us guessing (an old storyteller's trick, of course, and central to the craft), it also puts God at a distance, or at least seems to do so. For this is the first time we have heard of an apparent intermediary. God, it seems, is not dealing, perhaps cannot deal, directly with Hagar. He must send an intermediary, while he remains behind the half-closed doors of heaven. That, at least, is what the language most naturally suggests.

What is much more alarming, however, is the function that this mysterious 'messenger' seems to be playing. When the Israelites come out of Egypt, God will lead them to safety, and eventually bring the next generation into their promised land. Here God seems to be intervening to *prevent* escape, and to reinforce oppression. In Egypt God will smash the oppressor to pieces, and will finally see to the end of him at the Red Sea. Here, he blocks Hagar's way to freedom, stops her going home, and orders her back to the hand of her oppressor. The words, 'Go back to your mistress, and submit yourself to her abuse' are truly terrible. Whose side is this God on? Sarai's and Abram's, it would seem, and at Hagar's huge expense. God's supposed partiality, and the price to be paid for it by outsiders, have already become apparent in Genesis (see 12.10–20, for example, or the hints of what is to come in 12.6–7 or 13.14–17), and they will become even clearer in Exodus and beyond. This is the most disconcerting example of it to date. In the Old Testament as a whole we get used to expecting God to take the side of the oppressed against the oppressor. Here he seems to be aiding and abetting Sarai's cruelty, to be on the side of the slave-owner, however intolerable life may have been for the runaway slave. Furthermore, it is not entirely clear what purpose Hagar's return will serve, except to allow the narrator to emphasize Abram's being the father of the child when he is born, and to tell of him giving him a name (16.15–16). Sarai will get her slave back, of course, but that will turn out to be a very mixed blessing for all concerned.

Yet Hagar will not return as she left. She will go back with fine promises ringing in her ears, and heaven shining in her eyes.

> The messenger of YHWH said to her, 'I will increase, increase your offspring, until they are too many to count.'
> The messenger of YHWH said to her,
>
>> 'See now, you have conceived and will bear a son,
>> And you will call his name Ishmael,
>> For YHWH has heard the sound of your abuse.
>> He shall be a wild ass of a man,
>> His hand against everyone
>> And everyone's hand against him.
>> He shall be at odds with all his brothers.' (16.10–12)

This sounds like a different God! This God has a sharp ear for oppression, and does come to the aid of the oppressed after all! This God brings hope out of despair, and promises more than ever this slave-woman could have hoped for! This God turns things upside down, and makes an abused runaway slave into the ancestress of a great people! This God can create out of nothing! The voice of this God is only too familiar to anyone who has read through the stories of Abram and Sarai thus far. This is indeed the voice of YHWH, who has already promised Abram that his descendants will one day be past counting.

True, the promise given to Hagar says nothing of Hagarites. It does not give her her due. And the future it promises for her descendants is, at the very least, a highly ambiguous one. Not for them a Promised Land, nor a name of great renown and the political power to go with it. YHWH's words to Hagar about her son remind us too uncomfortably of the fate of Cain or Pride-and-joy in Genesis 4. They are not nearly as bright as the declaration God will make to Abraham in the next chapter:

> 'As for Ishmael, I have heard you.
> See, I have blessed him,
> I will make him fruitful,
> I will increase him exceedingly, exceedingly!
> He shall father twelve chieftains,
> And I will establish him as a great nation.' (17.20)

That is the language of Genesis 1, and of the original promises to Abraham in Genesis 12.2–3, and nearly matches the promises concerning Isaac and his descendants (see 17.16). By comparison, the promise to Hagar about her son seems dark indeed. And yet it also reminds us of the freedom given by God to the wild ass, or the wild ox and the horse, for that matter, in Job 39. And Claus Westermann would argue that it originated among the Ishmaelites themselves, and describes it as a 'jubilant, defiant affirmation of predatory, bedouin life'.[7] Defiant it surely is, and, here, in the wilderness of Shur, it must surely give divine sanction to Hagar's own defiance, and

54

support her in any future protest. If her son's divine destiny is to be 'a wild ass of a man', roaming free, and at no-one's beck and call, then surely Hagar is right to claim her own freedom, and cannot be meant to remain in slavery. She must return to Sarai and Abram, but only to wait till she can claim the larger freedom for which she was made, and which she will never again lose.

This is truly the voice of the God familiar to us from the bulk of the material in the Old Testament, and Hagar immediately recognizes it as such. Yet she not only hears. She *sees*. We, the hearers or readers of her story, can only listen. She, however, glimpses the one speaking. It is no mere messenger! It is God himself! The truth is out!

> She gave a name to YHWH who had spoken to her, 'You are El Roi, the God Who Sees![?]' For she thought, 'I have seen God after his seeing me![?]' (16.13)

The language here is all about seeing, though, unfortunately, the meaning of the name Hagar gives God is not entirely certain in the Hebrew, and what she thinks is even less so. Enough, however, is plain for us to be amazed at the honours heaped upon her in this story. Hers is the first annunciation scene in the Bible, and, of those select few who receive them, only she and the unnamed wife of Manoah in Judges 13 'see' God in the encounter. Hagar is, indeed, the first person in the Bible to be described as 'seeing' God, and only one other woman in the whole Bible, the unnamed wife of Manoah, will be accorded that privilege. No-one else at all gives a name to God.

We might well say she gives a name to a God who already has one, YHWH, and that is true. And yet that name is hidden in the heart of the divine, concealed within the dense mist where God is to be found (see Exodus 20.21). It cannot even be pronounced with any certainty, and to this day devout Jews refuse to try. In his translation of the book of Job Stephen Mitchell calls the God, the YHWH, who appears to Job in the whirlwind, 'The Unnameable'.[8] By those terms Hagar, and Hagar alone of all the myriads of characters of the Bible, dares to name the unnameable. God leaves her presence with a new identity. He is changed by this encounter.

The name she bestows upon him is enshrined in the one given to the spring or well that marks the spot:

> So they called the well Beer-lahai-roi, the Well of the Living One who Sees Me. (16.14)

God has been seen here, and the name is an eternal reminder of that.

What can it mean to 'see' God? The expression is rare in the Bible. Such vision is clearly thought out of the ordinary, and beyond expectation. Indeed, it is sometimes said to be impossible, or at least an experience impossible to survive (Exodus 33.20; John 1.18; and see also Exodus 3.6; Judges 13.22). To 'see' God is clearly to have an experience which is utterly overwhelming, shattering in its truth, its power and its mystery. Such experience lacks the naturalness of relations between God and human beings of which the Garden of Eden story speaks. And yet, of course, the language of seeing is the language of intimacy. Those who 'see' God find him very close at that moment. It is an attempt to sum up in a word the most profound sense of the closeness of God, the kind of experience that can most profoundly change us, and stay with us as an inspiration to the end of our lives. It is the language of heaven, for Paul will tell us that there we will see God face to face (1 Corinthians 13.12). It is the language of the Transfiguration story in the Gospels, of the resurrection appearances of Jesus, of the martyrdom of Stephen, or the Damascus road.

Beyond that there is little or nothing we can say. The language of 'seeing' God is itself an attempt to name the unnameable, to express what cannot be expressed, to use words where words so transparently fail us.

And who is this great figure who goes so deep into the truth of God at the spring at Beer-lahai-roi, and who leaves her mark upon him? She is a woman, a foreigner, a stranger, a slave, a runaway, a nobody, with a child in her womb of a man who has shown no concern for her, and a mistress whose cruelty has grown past her endurance!

Her encounter is so significant that it must reach the public domain. It turns the spot into a holy site and a place of worship for years to come. If you go to Israel today and ask to be shown the place, there will be those who believe they can tell you. (Later in Genesis, by a huge irony, Isaac – of all people, Isaac! – comes to live there (see 24.62; 25.11).)

However, Hagar is still a slave. She must return to Sarai, though the storyteller will not tell of the journey back to Mamre, only of the birth of her child, and of Abram taking for himself the privilege of naming him, when God in the desert promised that to Hagar herself.

At the end of this scene, much is left still unresolved: the relations between Hagar and Abram, and especially Hagar and Sarai; and the nature of God's commitment to Hagar. We have seen two very different pictures of God put side by side in this episode: God the secret policeman, God the agent of the slave-owner, finding a runaway slave and sending her back to the tyranny of her mistress, God deeply implicated in oppression and abuse; and, juxtaposed with that, God the source of blessing, God the giver of honour and hope beyond all expecting, who stamps his *nihil obstat* upon the attempt of the downtrodden to claim their freedom.

What kind of God is Hagar really dealing with? What kind of God are *we* dealing with? Those are the most important questions we are left with here. As far as Hagar is concerned, we will have to wait till Genesis 21 for them to be addressed again. That is the next time she appears on the stage of the narrative.

*   *   *

Again a crisis occurs. Again it arises out of the strain of Hagar's relations with Sarai, now renamed Sarah (as Abram is now Abraham), but this time it does not spring directly from a conflict between the two women. For now, miraculously, Sarah has a son of her own, Isaac, and there are new interests to be protected.

The child [Isaac] grew, and was weaned. Abraham made a great feast on the day Isaac was weaned. But Sarah saw the son of Hagar the Egyptian whom she had borne to Abraham playing Isaac. She said to Abraham, 'Chuck this slave-woman out, and her son! This slave-woman's son is not going to inherit along with my son, not with Isaac!' (21.8–10)

It was a dreadful business in Abraham's view – on account of his son. But God said to Abraham, 'Do not let this be such a bad business in your view – on account of the lad and your slave-woman. Whatever Sarah says to you, listen to her voice, for it is through Isaac that your offspring will be named after you. The son of the slave-woman also I will establish as a nation, for he too is your offspring.' (11–13)

So Abraham got up early in the morning, took some bread and a skin of water and gave them to Hagar. He put them on her shoulder, and the boy, and sent her away. She went and wandered about in the desert of Beer-sheba. (14)

The water from the skin was finished, and she cast the child underneath one of the bushes. She went and sat down by herself opposite him, about a bowshot's distance away, for she said, 'I cannot watch the child die.' She sat opposite him, lifted up her voice, and wept. (15–16)

God heard the boy's voice. The messenger of God called to Hagar from the heavens. He said to her, 'What is the matter, Hagar? Do not be afraid. God has heard the boy's voice where he is. Get up, take the boy, hold him tight with your hand, for I am going to establish him as a great nation.' (17–18)

God opened her eyes. She saw a well of water, and she went and filled the skin with water and gave the boy a drink. (19)

God was with the boy. He grew up and settled in the desert and became a master bowman. He settled in the desert of Paran, and his mother took him a wife from the land of Egypt. (20–1)

This is one of the most poignant stories in the Bible, told by a master storyteller. There is no romance, no sentimentality, nor any unnecessary detail. What incidental detail there is, and

58

it amounts to a good deal, is designed to arouse our feelings without letting them run away with us and make us forget the significance of the events.

In the very next chapter of Genesis we find the famous story of the near sacrifice of Isaac. There too, after hearing a speech from God, Abraham will get up early in the morning (22.3 begins in the Hebrew exactly as 21.14 does) and make preparations for a journey. That journey also will be towards a momentous encounter with God, and will end with words of promise. It too will be made by a lone parent and a child, and the child will come near to death. The parent will be Abraham himself, of course, the father. Here the child is accompanied by Hagar, his mother.

Why, then, when there are such striking similarities between the two episodes, when both stories are so compelling, written with such consummate skill, and quite clearly *meant* to be compared with one another, is one so much more famous than the other?

The answer is not hard to find. These stories are but parts of a much larger narrative that stretches all the way from Genesis 1 to the end of 2 Kings. That narrative begins as the story of creation and the universe, and continues for a spell as the story of humanity. But from Genesis 12 onwards it is the story of the people of Israel. Their ancestry is traced back to Abraham through Isaac, not to Hagar through Ishmael. Hagar and Ishmael quickly become superfluous to the plot, and so must disappear.

There is nothing wrong with that, of course. Storytellers must always focus their narrative upon relatively few characters, at the expense of others. The Hagarites must once have had their own stories of their origins, and told things differently. The trouble is, however, that in this story of Israel, Hagar and Ishmael become superfluous to the larger designs of God, also. They are but bystanders on the edge of his purposes. The mind of this God is focused on the descendants of Abraham and Sarah, not, except for two brief moments, on those of Abraham and Hagar.

The particular promises God gave to Abraham when first he

called him out of Mesopotamia are to be handed on to and by a single son. The religious and cultural upbringing of that son must not be threatened by contact with alien traditions. Abraham has two sons, and that is one too many. Moreover, one of those sons has an Egyptian mother. Hagar and Ishmael must go.

The story inhabits a world where mothers rather than fathers are responsible for educating children in the religious and cultural traditions of their people, at least when they live in foreign surroundings[9] (remember, neither Hagar, nor Sarah, who has come from Mesopotamia, is living among her own people). So Sarah, as the one responsible for Isaac's education, sees all this clearly, and much more readily than Abraham, who at first is bewildered by her command to get rid of Hagar and her son.[10] Moreover, for Sarah (and Isaac) there is a further complication. Ishmael is the elder of the two sons, and thus would normally inherit the finest that Abraham has to offer (at least such a practice was firmly established by the time the story reached the form in which we have it, and so would have helped to shape the response of its first hearers or readers). In Abraham's case, his finest does not lie in his herds nor his slaves, nor even his wives, but in the promises he has received from God. Ishmael, however, cannot inherit those, except only for the ones specifically related to himself and his own descendants. That has been made quite clear, by none other than God himself (see 17.15–21). Once Isaac is weaned, and thus has survived those first few years of infancy in which so many babies in that world died, Ishmael and his mother must go. When Sarah sees Ishmael 'playing Isaac', as the Hebrew puts it, acting the usurper, she realizes they must go quickly. They must go, not just for her sake, or because of Abraham and Isaac, but for the sake of the declared purposes of God. That is why God so readily agrees with Sarah, and tells Abraham to do what she says.

We now understand better why we seemed to have two different Gods in that earlier episode in chapter 16, and why the first became so implicated in oppression, as he does again here. The ancient Israelites had profound and highly developed

notions of a generous mercy and compassion in God, an unfail-
ing love, and a readiness to take the side of those in need.
Such a vision accorded with much of their own experience,
and is plain in the second account of Hagar's meeting with
God in the desert, and in the latter part of the first. And yet Israelite theology became intertwined with Israelite national pre-
judices and aspirations. There is always a danger that religious
people will prosecute their religion at other people's, or
peoples', expense. History, including that of the Christian
Church, is littered with such examples. So are parts of the Old
Testament, and the stories of Hagar having to leave Sarah and
Abraham's camp, and the beginning of her first encounter
with God, contribute to them. We have put our finger here
on one of the major limitations or flaws of the theology of the
Old Testament.

There are obvious similarities between the two stories of
Hagar in the desert, but also significant differences. In the first
she ran away, to claim her freedom, and to return home. In
the second she is forced to leave. She has no choice in the
matter, is able to take no initiative. Abraham takes some care
of her and her son this time, though he seems still to have
little or no feeling for her (he finds Sarah's abrupt order to
chuck out her slave and her child distressing 'on account of
his son'). But his provisions are entirely inadequate, and in
the harsh surroundings of the desert Hagar and her son face
death.

God does not come this time to stop Hagar in her tracks.
Hagar is not going anywhere. She is not striding purposefully
towards the Egyptian border. She is wandering about aim-
lessly, and she is lost, not knowing where she can find any
water to keep her son alive.

God does not come this time to submit Hagar to further
slavery and oppression. He comes to set her and her son free.
He comes to make the desert their home, not just a place
where they can return from the brink of death and survive in
the short term, but a place where they can flourish and over
time become a distinct and strong people.

In some respects this God seems more remote than before.

Hagar does not see him this time, and he calls to her 'from the heavens'. He belongs to another world, and seems to keep his distance. (We are reminded of the earlier Tower of Babel story in Genesis 11, where he 'goes down' to see what the people on the plain of Shinar are up to.) Nor does Hagar address him. There is no dialogue. Hagar only speaks to herself.

Yet the ambivalence of the theology of the first encounter is missing here. For all God's conniving with Abraham and Sarah in Hagar's banishment, the God who meets her in the desert this time is entirely on her side.

The divine promise concerning her son, given in the first encounter, is pronounced again, in a more positive, if briefer form. It is brief now because there are more urgent matters to attend to. The child is dying of thirst. If he dies, the promise dies with him. Water must be found and quickly. Ironically it has been there all the time, but Hagar has not seen it. Last time she left Sarah's and Abraham's camp a defiant woman, off to claim her destiny. Her head was held high and her eyes were wide open. Then she had no difficulty finding water in the desert, and she saw with unusual clarity. She saw God himself. Now she is a broken woman, blinded by despair and anticipated grief, unable to see the well she and her son have come to, and unwilling to see the tragedy that fills her eyes, the imminent death of her son.

God opens her eyes, and gives her back her son. He saves her from her own death, also, of course, but our minds are not focused on that, nor is hers, nor is God's. The storyteller paints a picture of a distraught mother, whose plight takes second place to that of her child. Indeed, so self-effacing is she, that the suffering of her son fills her world entirely. She has no thought for her own needs. Even when the well is shown to her, she gives her son a drink, and, within the bounds of the story, pays no heed to her own thirst. The picture is intensely moving, and perfectly realistic. A recent television programme showed a very young child who had suffered terrible injuries to his face from an attack by the family dog. The mother, holding him in her arms, said to the interviewer, 'You wish it were you, don't you.' That mother would understand Hagar and the way her story is written.

God's mind is where Hagar's is, with the distress of the child, with his survival, and his future. That is somewhat unnerving, of course. It is sons that matter in Genesis and beyond, and they have particular importance for the God of the narrative also. Another limitation and flaw in its theology. And yet still, in concentrating upon Ishmael, God is here only doing what this Hagar would wish of him. Furthermore, there is no doubt that God succeeds in restoring to Hagar not only her son and her ability to care for him, together with her own life, but also her dignity, her self-respect, and her old defiance. She is so damaged, so near to death when God finds her, that he must give her precise instructions what to do. But at the very end of this her story she seizes the initiative once more. She goes to Egypt to find a wife for her son. Egypt is no longer home. The desert is that. But Egypt is the place of her religious, cultural and ethical heritage. If that is to be retained for her son and his children, then a wife must be found for him who shares it herself. Hagar is as clear-sighted as Sarah was at Isaac's weaning feast. She knows what she must do for Ishmael, as Sarah knew what was necessary for Isaac. In fulfilling her duties, Hagar becomes the only woman in the Bible to choose a wife for her son.

We hear no more of Hagar. She departs from the narrative no longer a slave, but a free woman, who has found the particular freedom of the desert, who has taken charge of her destiny, and who bears the marks of not one but two close encounters with God. To her shrine at Beer-lahai-roi men and women, perhaps especially women, will come in the hope of finding what she found, and of seeing what she saw.

Today we do not need to go so far. We need only go on pilgrimage to the world of her remarkable stories.

6

God in the Dark

(Genesis 28.10–22; 32.22–32)

We may sometimes wish God to be straightforward. We may
be impatient with God's mystery, let alone his ambiguity. We
may wish to believe we know exactly where we stand with
her, and she with us. We may like to imagine we have walked
round God, and seen him from every angle. We may suppose
she holds no surprises for us any more, and be profoundly
grateful for that.

But ambiguity is what Genesis has already provided, in its
portrayal of its human characters, and also in its theology, and
we will find more of it as we explore two passages from the
Jacob cycle of stories. The God of the first episode will
unsettle us, as he did in the earlier part of that first story about
Hagar, while we will find the second passage one of the most
mysterious in the entire Bible. We will also discover that it is
one of the most profound.

Ambiguity, mystery and profundity go together, of course.
Those people who we suppose have no ambiguity about
them are but stereotypes of our imagining, satisfying our own
needs to canonize or demonize. A god who lacks mystery is
an idol. Genesis turns its back on idolatry, and though it does
not avoid stereotype entirely, it is particularly profound in its
characterization of human beings and its God, and in its treat-
ment of those moments when the human and the divine meet,
strike sparks from one another and set the world ablaze.

The Jacob cycle of stories is an especially long one. It
begins with his conception and birth in Genesis 25, and
ends, we might argue, with his death and burial at the end
of the book in chapter 50. On that score it falls into two
parts, divided by two genealogies listing the sons of Jacob

himself and the descendants of his brother Esau (35.22b—
36.43).

In the first part Jacob is primarily son, brother, nephew,
husband. Children are born to him, but his relations with
them are not explored. Instead, the stories concern his relationships with his mother Rebekah, with his father Isaac, his
brother Esau, his uncle Laban, or his wives Leah and Rachel.

In the second part he is simply father. The stories there are
about him and his sons, though one son, Joseph, quickly
takes centre stage, and occupies it for so much of the action
that we usually refer to the last fourteen chapters of Genesis
as the Joseph story, not the second half of the Jacob one.
Indeed, those chapters spend most of their time on Joseph's
relations with his brothers, rather than on his relationship
with Jacob, and most of the action takes place in Egypt,
with Jacob still in Canaan. Yet even there we are never
allowed to forget Jacob for long, and the terrible song of his
grief for the son he believes he has lost can always be heard
in the background, till the truth of Joseph's survival is out
and tears are shed at their reunion. In that part of his story
tables are turned, and Jacob himself becomes the victim of a
most fearful deceit. He now is the father duped by his sons,
just as Isaac was once so cruelly deceived by him and
Rebekah. The brothers trick him into thinking his favourite
son, Joseph, is dead (37.29–36). Yet he is not humiliated by
the deception. He retains his authority as head of the family,
even over Joseph when he becomes second in command to
the great pharaoh in Egypt (and that means, in the world of
the story, the second most powerful man on earth). When
eventually he comes down to Egypt, he is given an audience
with the pharaoh, and we see him not prostrating himself
before him, as we would expect, but giving him his blessing
(47.7, 10)! His own deathbed scene parallels that of his
father, Isaac, yet is quite different. He had made a fool out of
Isaac, and tricked him into giving him the blessing prepared
for his elder brother Esau (chapter 27[1]). Now, when his own
sight is failing and he is near to death, and he is himself presented with two grandsons for blessing, he remains in

complete control and ensures that the younger of the two
receives the larger promises for the future, despite Joseph's
attempts to have it otherwise (chapter 48). This last section
of Genesis, which has repeatedly anticipated Jacob's death
(see 37.25; 42.38; 43.27–8; 44.22, 29, 31; 45.9, 13, 28; 46.30),
spends far longer on it when it arrives than on Joseph's
(47.29—50.14, compared with just 50.24–6 on Joseph). Thus
there is a sense in which it remains Jacob's tale to the end,
and the Jacob we find in these final fourteen chapters of
Genesis, for all the disastrous favouritism he shows towards
Joseph, is conspicuous for his dignity, his authority, and in
the end his nobility.

The Jacob of the first part of his story is much more complex:
clever, though not as clever as his mother; a trickster who
tricks his brother, his father, and his uncle, and each time
wins; a usurper who gains the birthright and the blessing due
to Esau, who takes his brother's place beside the deathbed of
his father, and who, much later, runs away from his uncle
Laban with far more of his possessions than Laban had
planned for.

In those moments of understandable folly when we suppose
that we have to be good in order to enter the presence of
God, we might expect the God of these stories to wait till
Jacob has settled into the dignity of his old age, before
deigning to meet with him. The truth of Genesis is different.
Of the eight occasions when God appears to, or speaks with
Jacob, only one occurs in those last fourteen chapters (28.10–
22; 31.3; 31.10–13; 32.1–2; 32.22–31; 35.1; 35.9–15; 46.1–4),
and the two most remarkable encounters take place when
Jacob is up to his neck in deceit. The first of them happens
as he is fleeing from Esau because he has tricked him out of
Isaac's deathbed blessing. The second comes during his
return from twenty years with his uncle Laban, after a series
of episodes full of rumbustious humour, when we have had
two tricksters, Jacob and Laban, on stage at once, and have
seen first one, then the other get the upper hand. It is these
two encounters which are the subject of the rest of this
chapter.

Jacob set out from Beer-Sheba and travelled towards Haran. He chanced upon a certain place and spent the night there, for the sun had gone. He took one of the stones of the place, set it up for his head, and in that place lay down. (28.10–11)

He had a dream. See, a stairway stood upon the earth! The head of it touched the heavens, and see, messengers of God going up and down upon it! And see, YHWH stood beside him and said, 'I am YHWH, the God of Abraham your father, and the God of Isaac. The land on which you lie I give to you and to your descendants. Your descendants will be like the dust of the earth, and will expand to the sea, to the east, to the north, to the Negeb. All the families of the earth will find blessing in you and in your descendants. And see, I am with you. I will watch over you wherever you travel, and I will bring you back to the land, for I will not leave you till I have done what I have spoken of to you.' (12–15)

Jacob woke from his sleep and said, 'Heavens above! YHWH is in this place, and I did not know!'

He was awestruck, and said, 'How awesome is this place! This is none other than the House of God, and this the Gate of Heaven!'

Jacob got up early in the morning, and took the stone he had set up for his head, set it up as a sacred pillar, and poured oil on its head. He called the name of that place Beth-El (but Luz was the original name of the town).

Jacob vowed a vow, saying, 'If God is with me and watches over me on this journey I am making, and gives me bread to eat and clothes to wear, and if I return in peace to my father's house, and YHWH is my God, then this stone that I have set up as a sacred pillar will be the House of God, and of all that you give to me I shall give a tenth, a tithe to you.' (16–22)

It is, of course, the famous story of Jacob's ladder, though it would, perhaps, be more appropriate to call it the story of God's stairway.

Each of Jacob's eight meetings with God happens during the course of a journey, or else results in him moving on. In this case Jacob is on his way out of God's Land, on a journey of nearly three hundred miles to Haran. When God meets him twenty years later at the Jabbok, he will be on his way back to the Land. It is as if God meets him each time as he approaches the border, like a border guard checking, or rather, since he is God, awarding him his credentials. A God at or near the border is not so very strange. Such a God appears in tales more ancient than Genesis,[2] and for some of us he still meets us on our own travels. For we also have sacred places or holy lands, and we know what it is to meet God on their borders, and to have a sense of leaving him behind when we depart. That is how it is, for all our clear understanding that God does not reside in any particular spot more than in any other.

Like the encounter at the Jabbok, this one happens at night. The *sun* has gone, and we will not hear mention of it again till the end of the Jabbok story. That is no accident. The author or compiler of these stories pays attention to such details, and means us to compare the two incidents, as indeed we have begun to do already. He (I think it is he, not she[3]) means us also to understand Jacob as spending the twenty years in between them in the 'darkness' of a foreign land.

Yet what is this darkness of which the storyteller speaks here, in this as yet uncertain place on the way to Haran? Is it simply the darkness of night? Is it just an indication of the belief, widespread in the ancient Near East, and significant for the story of Joseph later on in Genesis, that God can communicate with human beings in a particularly powerful way through dreams? Might we believe that the human mind, unconstrained by its usual mundane inhibitions, is given by sleep a particular freedom to enter the strange world of God? Or is this darkness the 'dense mist where God is', to borrow that brilliant phrase from Exodus 20.21, that darkness designed both to make the light of God's glory bearable to the human eye, and to demonstrate his mystery? Or, on another level, is this the darkness of Jacob's fear and despair?

Whichever it is (and why do we need to choose?, the story

allows any of these interpretations), make no mistake about it, Jacob is at his most vulnerable here, as he will be again at the Jabbok. He has a long and dangerous journey ahead of him, and a brother out for his blood behind him. What lies ahead in Haran, he does not know. He has been told by Rebekah, his mother, to go there till Esau quietens down and it is safe for him to return (27.42–5). His father, Isaac, has sent him on his way with fine words of blessing, and with instructions to 'take a wife' for himself from among the daughters of Laban, Rebekah's brother (28.1–5). However, what it will be like for him when he gets there, if he gets there, he does not yet know. If he obeys Isaac's instructions, Laban's daughters will have little or no say in the matter. We and Jacob himself can be sure of that. But Laban will. How much will ties of blood count with him? (Not very much as it will turn out, for though Laban will give him not one, but two of his daughters in marriage, in other respects he will treat him as a hired hand.) And how long will it take for Esau's anger to cool? (As it transpires, because Laban will keep Jacob working for him for twenty years, it will have time not only to disappear altogether, but turn itself into startling magnanimity, as their reunion in chapter 33 will show.) For the time being Jacob seems to have nothing.

Admittedly, in two separate acts of blessing Isaac has spoken of God giving him 'the dew of the heavens, the fat of the earth, an abundance of corn and new wine'; of peoples serving him, tribes prostrating themselves before him, and his brothers doing the same; of God making him and his descendants so fruitful that they will become 'a host of peoples'; of him and his descendants inheriting the land promised to Abraham and to Isaac himself (27.28–9; 28.3–4). By the time we reach Beth-El, however, such splendid words seem to count for very little. The beginnings of their fulfilment seem hardly possible, or at best a very distant prospect. For the moment Jacob has nothing but his fear. In his vow at the end of this passage he will voice his hope that God will provide him with protection and with food and clothing on his journeys and in Haran. Clearly, he is fully aware of his vulnerability and of his destitution. He seems to have little expectation of much kindness from Laban. By his own reckoning he will have to rely on God for his very survival.

To such a Jacob God appears. That should not surprise us. In the Old Testament God has a sharp eye for those in desperate need, and a habit of coming to their aid. We have seen that already with Hagar. Furthermore, before even Jacob and his twin Esau were born, God assured Rebekah that each would be the ancestor of a nation, and that Jacob, though born after Esau, would gain supremacy over him (25.23). The words of Isaac's blessings are in accord with these divine intentions. Jacob only needs to hear the promises from God himself, as Abraham and Isaac did, and that is what, in his dream at a certain place on the way to Haran, he does. They are bright promises for the distant future, promises with no strings attached, and reassuring ones, also, for the days and months, and, as it turns out, the years, that lie immediately ahead. 'See, I am with you. I will watch over you wherever you travel, and I will bring you back to the land, for I will not leave you till I have done what I have spoken of to you.'

That is precisely what Jacob needs to hear. That is what anyone needs to hear. 'I am with you.' Just two words in the Hebrew, two words which return us to Eden, which answer our ancient yearnings and provide the only sure foundation for hope. Jacob cannot ask for more. And yet he is given it. He is given the vision of a stairway linking heaven and earth, alive with the messengers of God. Many people seem these days to live in a world where heaven seems so remote that it is no longer conceivable, and where lines of communication between them and God are not even contemplated. This world with all its ambiguities, and this life with death as its sure conclusion are all there is. Hence the prevailing busyness, the transparent fear of mortality, the striving for impossible perfection, the readiness to heap blame and to punish when that is not achieved. Jacob, by contrast, finds himself on the edge of heaven, and with no great chasm fixed between, but stairs that he might climb. This is not just an assurance of heaven's existence, of there being another dimension to things, another world where God is to be found. Such an assurance might seem enough, but Jacob's vision offers a heaven whose door is open, and whose realms are accessible. More even than that, this heaven is coming down to earth, at least to Jacob's patch of ground. Jacob does not need to climb God's stairway. God's messengers are going up and down upon it. This heaven, therefore, is not silent either. This heaven is prepared to speak, to tell the Truth. What more could anyone ask, except for God's intimate presence? Jacob is granted that also!

Though we have remarked upon the power of the words 'I am with you' to take us back to Eden, we may seem at first to be some way from it here. The coming of God to this place on the borders of the Promised Land is shrouded in mystery. God comes in the dark, and his coming is remarkable, lacking the seeming inevitability of the Garden. Jacob speaks of his need for clothing, but we cannot conceive of this God cutting and stitching, as he did for the man and woman in the Garden. He comes also when Jacob is asleep, unable to reply or engage in dialogue. And yet the intimacy of Eden is still largely recovered, for God does not call to Jacob from heaven, as he did that second time to Hagar (21.17), but comes down the stairway himself. He stands beside the sleeping Jacob, not a God incarnate, admittedly, but still a God down to earth, attending carefully to a human being and his great need. No wonder this story is so famous! It goes so unerringly to the heart of our deepest longings.

No wonder, either, that Jacob is so overwhelmed by it all when he wakes up! Hagar gave a new name to the God who met her in the desert the first time. Jacob does not dare do that, but he does rename the place. *Now* we learn where this 'certain place' is! Now we learn that Jacob has been in a Canaanite town all the time! For this storyteller Luz is a complete nonentity till the moment of Jacob's encounter with God, and till he gives it its new name, Beth-El, the House of God. It was left to others, it seems, to turn Hagar's well into the pilgrimage site of Beer-lahai-roi. In this story, however, Jacob himself sets up a sacred pillar, and vows that if he returns safely from Haran, then he will found a cult at Beth-El and ensure its funding.

The stone that lay at his head during the dream is turned into a mark of the encounter. Parts of Britain are littered with ancient standing stones, quietly marking the sacred and the finding of it. But in their case we can get little further towards unlocking their secrets, for they were left behind by a non-literate people, and the stories attached to them have long since been forgotten. The stone at Beth-El, however, still speaks. The very word for it in the Hebrew is eloquent, for it is *matstsebah*, and that recalls the stairway which 'stood' (*mutstsab*) upon the earth, and the God who 'stood' (*nitstsab*) beside Jacob. The three words are from the same root. Further-more, the stone has its 'head' anointed with oil, like a king. That word, too, serves as a double reminder, first of the stairway, with its 'head' in the heavens, and secondly of Jacob who set it at his 'head' before going to sleep.[4] Thus the stone borrows its sanctity not just from God, but from Jacob. It is the very stone he put beside his head! One can almost hear the sudden hush in the voice of the guide showing pilgrims round the sanctuary at Beth-El! In the Mosque of the Ascension on the top of the Mount of Olives in Jerusalem they will show you with tired solemnity the 'imprint of Jesus' foot', caught in stone as he was in the act of ascending to heaven! Like the well at Beer-lahai-roi, Jacob's stone attempts to mark the footsteps of God, though in a way that fortunately is more oblique. Like the well, it seeks also to commemorate a particular encounter. The well is the one 'where Hagar met with God and gave him a name'. The standing stone is the one 'that lay against Jacob's head in his dream'. And just as pilgrims went to Beer-lahai-roi in the hope of seeing what Hagar once saw, so they will now come to Beth-El, the House of God, hoping, perhaps expecting, to discover God standing beside them with words of hope and comfort.

We might imagine from a quick reading of this passage that the encounter belongs entirely to the time of the dream, and that Jacob wakes in the morning to find God has disappeared together with the stairway and its messengers. Yet the famous words he speaks when he wakes up and also his last words in the passage show that this is not so. 'Heavens above! The Lord *is* in this place, and I did not know!' he says when he wakes, not, 'The Lord *was* in this place.' He speaks of the present, not of the hours that have gone. God is still beside him. That is why at the end of his solemn vow, though most of its lines speak of God in the third person, he suddenly turns and addresses him direct. His sleep made dialogue impossible. Now he is awake, however, he can respond. '. . . of all that *you* give to me I shall give a tenth, a tithe to *you*'. Hitherto he has been more conspicuous for his taking. Now, after this first meeting with God, he speaks of giving. He will do the same after the Jabbok, when he will offer back to Esau the blessing he once stole from him.[5]

'But wait a minute,' we might say. 'It is all very well for Jacob. What about Isaac and Esau? Jacob has tricked them out of the giving or receiving of blessing, and has grievously humiliated them both in the process. Never mind God's promise to Rebekah, Jacob is a cruel cheat, prepared to deceive his own father on his deathbed, and rob his brother of his dignity and honour! *This* is the kind of man God meets here with his rare intimacy and fine words of comfort! What about Isaac and Esau? What kind of God is this who rewards deceit, and rubs salt into the wounds of the injured? A God, it seems, who lifts up the powerful on their thrones, and brings down the lowly!'

We are back again with that same flaw in Israelite theology we detected while considering God's first meeting with Hagar. We saw her left as a bystander on the edge of the purposes of God, because her son Ishmael was not the child of God's larger promises to Abraham. So with Esau. His descendants will be the Edomites, not the people of Israel. As far as the promises of God to Abraham and Isaac are concerned, Esau is an awkward irrelevance, or rather an obstacle to be overcome. Jacob must be the one to carry the promises, though he is the younger of the two brothers. Never mind his not deserving the role, he has been set aside for it from before he was born, and by hook or by crook he must play it.

Yet that, of course, is only to explain, not to excuse. Admittedly, there is hope for us here, more hope than if Jacob had deserved what he received. There is a glimpse, perhaps more than a glimpse, perhaps a bright vision, of that surprising generosity and prodigality that always accompany the grace of God. It is not the good who are saved, but the sinners. We Christians have been trying to say that for a long time, and it is a major theme of both Testaments in our Bibles. Yet when Heather McKay says of this story in Genesis 28, 'the reader still has the feeling that crime does pay',[6] this particular reader has to agree with her. In the end we are left disconcerted as well as encouraged by this passage. This was not what Abraham had in mind in that passionate pleading of his for the people of Sodom. True, he was arguing there that God's mercy should transcend the demands of justice. But not at the further expense of the victims of injustice. Quite the reverse. Abraham was concerned that the victims of human beings' cruelty should not suffer more at the hands of God. At Beth-El, however, that is precisely what seems to happen to Isaac and Esau. The salt of God's partiality is rubbed into the open wounds left by Jacob's theft of their honour. Abraham's remarkable vision of how God might exercise justice was destroyed in the burning of Sodom and the other cities of the Dead Sea plain. Hagar was sent by God back to the cruel abuse of her mistress. Now for a third time God's justice seems to be found wanting.

At least with Hagar the matter found some resolution. We did not find God's second meeting with her begging the same theological questions as the first. In the stories of Jacob might we find things, if not put straight, at least adjusted at the Jabbok?

*   *   *

Twenty years pass by. Twenty years before Jacob is able to go home. It is not because it takes that long for Esau to simmer down. In his uncle Laban, Jacob, the trickster, the deceiver, the heel-catcher[7] meets his match. Laban is not having any of Jacob's usual tricks. When Jacob tries to marry his daughter,

Rachel, with her older sister Leah still unmarried, Laban swops the two women over on the wedding night, leaving Jacob to realize his mistake when the next morning comes! Seven years' labour is the price Jacob has to pay for marrying the daughter he has not chosen, and seven years more for the one he loves. All those years, and for six more, Laban treats him like a hired hand, cheats on him, cuts his wages ten times, and tries to ensure he does not amass any wealth of his own. Jacob's own native trickery, though at times wonderful to behold, is not quite up to all this. In the end he does win over Laban and departs for Canaan a wealthy man, but only because God has come to his rescue (see 30.30; 31.3, 5, 7, 13, 16, 24, 29, 42). Ultimately, Laban's trickery is not enough either. He comes hard up against the promises of God. At Beth-El God assured Jacob he would be with him, to protect and provide for him. This has hardly meant that Jacob has had an easy time of it in Haran. The God of Genesis is not a God who removes all obstacles and brings instant solutions on demand, and he is not Jacob's slave. Yet promises are promises, and Jacob cannot be left to see out his days in penury in Haran. He must make his escape, back to Canaan, to the land of the promises of God.

And so he does, with Rachel and Leah, eleven sons and a daughter, male and female slaves, camels and donkeys and large flocks of sheep and goats, and, thanks to Rachel, Laban's household gods for good measure. Laban pursues him, as one day the pharaoh of Egypt will chase the fleeing Israelites. He gets him in a corner, as the pharaoh will hem in the Israelites by the Red Sea. But the pharaoh will not prevail then, and nor does Laban now. Rachel's cleverness (see the hilarious episode of 31.33–5) and, beneath it all, God's partiality defeat him. 'As God's protege,' says Jan Fokkelman, '[Jacob] goes away, a victor; he is unassailable and he knows it.'[8]

'He is unassailable and he knows it.' Perhaps, but though Laban is no longer to be reckoned with, Esau is. Back in 27.42–5 Rebekah told Jacob to stay with Laban till she sent word to him to say it was safe to come home. But no word has arrived. For all Jacob knows, Esau is still out for his blood. He travels back towards Canaan, a prodigal son who left terrible hurt and boiling anger behind him when he went to Haran twenty years before, terrified of the welcome he might receive. He expects the worst, and, as he draws near the boundaries of the Land, begins to make elaborate plans to try to placate his brother. As it will turn out, his efforts are unnecessary. But Jacob does not know that, and he journeys on feeling anything but unassailable. Yet promises are promises, and God's promises are surely so. The stone at Beth-El stands as a witness to them.

God's messengers meet him on the way (32.1). Once again God takes him by surprise. 'This is God's camp!' he cries, and gives the place a new name, 'Mahanaim', or 'Two Camps'. There are echoes here of the mystery of Beth-El, of that earlier unexpected encounter with God near the border, of Jacob then coming to his senses and realizing where he was, of the giving of a name to evoke a sense of what had taken place. Yet if we think this is the true parallel to the Beth-El story, we are mistaken. This tiny episode of just two verses (32.1–2) is but the curtain-raiser. The real drama is yet to begin.

Jacob sends his own messengers ahead to tell Esau of his return, to seize the initiative and to try to win his brother over. The messengers return with the news that Esau is coming to meet him with four hundred men. Four hundred! Jacob is horrified. He assumes Esau is out for terrible revenge, and lays his fear open to God in prayer, reminding him of the promises he made at Beth-El (32.6–12).

He splits his flocks and herds into three and sends them on ahead at intervals with his male slaves to meet up with Esau on the way, and, he hopes, put him in a better mood. He hedges his bets. God has already got him out of some tight corners, and he has just prayed urgently to him for his support. Better not rely on him entirely, however. Use some bribery, just in case. Three very substantial bribes, one after the other. If God does not do the trick, they just might!

And so he reaches the Jabbok, a gorge running from the east into the Jordan. After this there will be no going back. This is Jacob's Rubicon.

It is night. Again it is night, and again God will come to Jacob. But this time he will not stand beside him. He will get to grips with him and wrestle with him till just before the dawn! Is this also a dream? Is it just a vision? But what kind of dream or vision can leave someone with a permanent limp at the end (for that is what Jacob will have)? We enter here upon one of the most mysterious and compelling stories of encounter with God in all Scripture.

> Jacob got up that night. He took his wives, his two maids and his eleven children and crossed the crossing of the Jabbok. He took them and crossed them over the river, and then crossed over his belongings. Jacob was left on his own. (32.22–24a)
>
> A man wrestled with him till the rising of the dawn. (24b)
>
> He saw he was unable to prevail against him, so he touched the socket of his thigh. The socket of Jacob's thigh was dislocated as he wrestled with him. He said, 'Let me go, for the dawn has risen!'
>
> But he replied, 'I will not let you go unless you bless me.'
>
> He said to him, 'What is your name?'
>
> He said, 'Jacob.'
>
> He said, 'Not as Jacob, Heel-catcher, will your name be known from now on, but as Israel, God-fighter, for you have fought with God and with human beings, and have prevailed.'
>
> Jacob then asked and said, 'Tell me, please, your name.'
>
> He replied, 'Now why do you ask my name?' And there he blessed him. (25–9)
>
> Jacob called the name of the place Peniel, Face-of-God, 'For' [he said] 'I have seen God face to face, and my life has been saved!'
>
> The sun rose on him as he crossed Penuel, limping on his thigh. (30–1)

Jacob is once more on his own here, as he was at Beth-El. During the wrestling bout it is as if his wives and children and maids are out of sight and out of earshot. When earlier the stairway was set up between heaven and earth, and the messengers of God took themselves up and down upon it, and God came and stood beside Jacob, it was as if the inhabitants of Luz were a world away. And so they were. They were so far removed from what was taking place, that even the name of their town was not mentioned till it was almost all over, not until it had been changed to Beth-El! Though Jacob's experience was set to come into the public sphere with that change of name and with the establishment of a cult there, nevertheless, in the first place, the place of the story, there was something essentially private about it. So too with the encounter at the Jabbok. On the one hand it turns out to be so significant that the people of God will take their very name, Israel, from it, and will commemorate it in one of their food laws (32.32 explains that they avoid eating the sinew attached to the hip joint, because God touched Jacob there). On the other hand this is a meeting between God and one man. It is Jacob's experience, and his alone. During the night it has reality only for him. As the deepest experience always is, it is an essentially private matter.

It is dark. Once again it is dark. Once again God appears in the night. Again we find ourselves asking how many kinds of dark this is. It is most certainly 'the dense mist where God is', that awesome obscurity that hides his very identity and allows him to pose at first as a human being. Surely it is also the darkness of Jacob's fear and apprehension.

This time the darkness is one of Jacob's own choosing. At Beth-El he lay down to sleep before the vision came. Here he has got up, unable perhaps to sleep. This time he is awake. That, of course, makes the episode much more extraordinary. We cannot explain it as a nightmare with an unexpectedly happy ending. This wrestling match is for real!

Where exactly it takes place is left uncertain. The story begins with repeated crossings. Four times the word 'cross' is used to emphasize the significance of what Jacob is doing. The Jabbok represents the border. Once across he cannot go back. But precisely where he is when he is 'left on his own' is not explained. On which bank is he, or is he on neither, but in midstream? And which way is he going? Realizing the significance of the Jabbok, is he funking it at the last minute? Is he deserting and running away? Is he facing the way he has come, when the mysterious figure of the night meets him and stops him in his tracks? Or, as Jan Fokkelman prefers,[9] is he now determined not to hide behind his entourage any more, but face his brother and take the consequences? We cannot tell. The writing is too sparse, particularly at the beginning. Nowhere, in fact, does the story give an answer. It is part of its intrigue.

Another part is its silence on the matter of the purpose of the wrestling bout. Hermann Gunkel tells us it is 'obviously a matter of life and death'.[10] But Gunkel is too much influenced by tales of demons attacking unwary travellers that he finds lurking beneath the text of Genesis.[11] From the text as we have it, it is not obvious at all that the one who wrestles with Jacob is out to kill him, or even injure him, or that Jacob has any violent intent on his part. Maybe this is sport, God's *play*! Perhaps God is more partner than assailant. When Jacob is given his new name Israel, we hear then of fighting, for the name means 'God-fighter', and Jacob is told he has 'fought' with God and with human beings. Yet still the storyteller fails to tell us the purpose of this particular 'fight', let alone give any hint that it is meant as a fight to the death.

It would seem, at least, that it demands extraordinary strength, skill, determination and stamina from Jacob, for the bout lasts till the dawn, and Jacob has the better of it, although his opponent is God himself! Back in Haran, when first he arrived, he rolled a stone off the mouth of a well for Rachel and her flock, when normally it took the combined shoving of all the local shepherds to do it (29.1–10). Before that we witnessed him setting upright the stone at Beth-El, which would probably have been nearly seven feet high.[12] Jacob is plainly a man of very unusual physical strength. But rolling a stone off a well's mouth, however large, and setting upright a seven foot menhir all by oneself can hardly be called adequate preparation for wrestling with God through the small hours of the night!

Yet, in fact, as the bout continues, it is not plain to what extent physical strength is involved at all. The touch from

God that threatens to turn the fight is but that, a 'touch'. Some of our versions speak of God 'striking' Jacob on the thigh, but that is to misrepresent the Hebrew. The hip joint is dislocated, sure enough, but it is dislocated by a mere touch!

Indeed, one of the striking things about this story is its comparative avoidance of the language of violence. In the end it becomes not a matter of holds, or falls, or submissions, but of words. The result is decided, remarkably, not by the dislocation of Jacob's hip, but by a series of questions and answers. We might have expected Jacob to curl up in immediate agony after his hip was put out of joint, but he carries on as if nothing has happened, and, moreover, the beginning of the dialogue which follows makes it plain he still has the upper hand. The end of it all comes not with pain, though Jacob will leave the Jabbok with a limp, but with blessing and the rising of the sun that set for so long at Beth-El.

At what point in all this does Jacob realize who he is wrestling with? Another question, and yet more intrigue and room for the imagination! After the episode at Beth-El we might think he only realizes at the end, when the dawn comes and it is all over. We might find a sudden recognition of God in his exclamation, 'I have seen God face to face!' Or did he see much earlier, when he asked for a blessing? Perhaps it was only a suspicion then. Perhaps suspicion became realization when the blessing was finally given. Surely it is reasonable to suppose the nature of the blessing betrayed its source.

Yet the timing of the recognition is relatively unimportant. What matters is that Jacob arrives at it, and that we do also, the readers and hearers of the story. After 'I have seen God face to face!' there can be no room for doubt. That talk at the beginning of 'a man' wrestling with Jacob misled us, and no doubt Jacob himself, who must have thought it was Esau, or one of his brother's men.

The complete text of the exclamation runs, 'I have seen God face to face, and my life has been saved!' Some translations suggest, '... and *yet* my life has been saved'. The Hebrew can bear that sense, and some might say it is encouraged by sentiments such as that in Exodus 33.20, where God says to Moses, 'You cannot see my face, for no-one can see my face and live.'[13] By that token we can expect Jacob to be amazed that he has survived at all. However, he may not mean saved from the encounter with God. He may mean saved from Esau and all that threatens him. He may mean that he is safe now after all the trials of the past and the great uncertainties of the future. He might mean he has found salvation, a kind of resurrection, light where there was only darkness, hope where before there was panic and near despair.

We have said this wrestling bout is not presented to us as a dream, though as it proceeds it may seem more and more like one. It is for real. But what kind of reality are we talking about? What is the reality of a wrestling bout through the small hours of the night with God? What can it mean to speak of such things?

First we must remember this is storytelling. It is not mere reportage. It is very close to poetry, for it captures so much in such a small space. Ultimately the source of this story must be looked for in religious experience. It conjures up in remarkably few words something of the character of those rare, mysterious encounters with God that change human beings and mark them for life. Perhaps the original storyteller was attempting to convey the strange paradox, the awesome power, the unexpected blessing of such an experience of his or her own. In entering the story, we dare to enter the world of that experience. We ourselves risk leaving with its mark upon us, with a blessing granted just when we were not expecting it, and with a new sense of identity.

The question this passage raises for theology is, what are the *consequences* of speaking of God like this? To that it does allow some ready answers.

It gives us a picture of an extraordinarily intimate God. This God has his hands on Jacob! The two of them are locked in struggle for hours on end! We have not seen God at such close quarters with a human being since the creation of the man and the woman in Eden. We will not see God at such very close quarters again in Scripture.

It tells of a God incarnate, for he meets with Jacob in the form of 'a man'.

It speaks, as almost no other Old Testament passage does, of God's vulnerability. For the story represents Jacob as having the upper hand till he is asked his name and reveals himself as the Heel-catcher. And when, after that, God gives him his new name and explains it for him, he tells him he has fought with human beings and with God, and *has prevailed*! Such language seems impossible. It could only come from story-telling or poetry. The makers of doctrine, or the authors of careful theological treatises, could never allow it. For them it is altogether too elusive, too wild and dangerous, this 'you have prevailed'. How does this storyteller mean us to take it? Are we meant to see a mischievous gleam in his God's eye? Are we meant to catch in its tones the sounds of God's exasperation, or the echoes of his pain? Once again, we are given no directions. Typically the storyteller leaves us free to make up our own minds. It is part of the genius and the generosity of the work. Yet surely we can say we will not find another image of God's vulnerability quite as striking as this till we reach Golgotha.

As far as Jacob and Jacob's God is concerned, the story of the Jabbok goes some way towards setting the record of Beth-El straight. There it seemed Jacob had it too easy. His cruel deceiving of his father and brother met too quickly with the comfort of God's presence and the reassurance of his promises. At the Jabbok, despite the comparative absence of the language of violence, we can hardly say that Jacob has it easy! We cannot be sure that God comes to knock the stuffing out of him, for, as we have seen, the fight's purpose is not explained. Yet it is most certainly a story of struggle, a long and awesome struggle, struggle with God himself. As Jan Fokkelman remarks, 'here the Heel-catcher is caught'.[14] Jacob is forced to face up to his God, and face also the question of his own identity. The struggle is not just with God, but with himself. He is taught a lesson at the Jabbok, that gaining blessing by tripping people up will not do for the bearer of the promises of God. As God said to him at Beth-El, he is to be a source of blessing for all the families of the earth, a *giver* of blessing, not one who snatches it for himself whenever he can get it. That is why God does not bless him at the Jabbok at the point in the bout where he demands it. He blesses him later, when he, and we ourselves, the hearers of the story, are not expecting such a thing. Jacob must learn that blessing has to be given freely, not extorted. With the hindsight given by the Jabbok story, we can see that God was teaching him that at Beth-El also, but our concern for Isaac and Esau made it hard to see at the time.

That goes some way to setting the record straight. But Isaac's and Esau's humiliation remain. The storyteller has tried to restore some dignity to Isaac by having him choose of his own free will to bless and instruct Jacob before he sets off for Haran (28.1–5), and he will do the same for Esau by awarding him such magnanimity, such extraordinary brotherly love in the account of his reunion with Jacob in chapter 33. Beyond that, however, he cannot go. The partiality of Jacob's God will not allow him.

These remain magnificent, but flawed, stories.

7

An Expert Intervenes

(Genesis 37—50)

Genesis 37—50! It looks as though this will be a long chapter! In fact, it will be one of the shorter ones, for there is almost nothing to report, no great encounter with God to explore, such as we have been finding hitherto. Indeed, we will discover that the very absence of any meeting with God will be one of the more significant features of this famous part of Genesis.

In the opening chapter of this last section of Genesis, this second part of the tale of Jacob, or the story of Joseph, as it is most commonly called, God is not even referred to. There are several places where we might have expected a mention. Joseph has two dreams, but he does not speak of them coming from God. Later he will tell Pharaoh in Egypt that two dreams he has received are a means of communication used by God to show him what he is about to do (41.25, 28, 39), but there is no such talk here. In Genesis 25.22–3 Rebekah learned from God that the older of her two sons would end up serving the younger, but now that Joseph, the second youngest of Jacob's sons, tells his brothers the time will come when they will bow down before him, we are left not knowing whether his predictions have the divine *imprimatur* or not.

Secondly, when his brothers are out with the flocks and Joseph is instructed by Jacob to find them, he is told their whereabouts by a man who finds him wandering about in the fields. The man knows where they are, because he overheard the brothers discussing their plans. When, much later in the Genesis—Kings narrative, Saul's father's donkeys go missing, Saul and his servant consult no passing stranger, but 'a man of God'. They go out of their way to meet with him, and find themselves speaking with the great Samuel himself (1 Samuel 9.1–14). Samuel predicts that when they leave, two men will meet them by Rachel's tomb and give them further information about the donkeys, and that this meeting will be a sign from God (10.1–2). There is no mention anywhere of divine guidance in Joseph's search for his brothers. The man Joseph meets is simply one of the locals; his information signifies nothing at all (or so, at least, it would seem) beyond the sharpness of his hearing.

His brothers see Joseph coming. Some of them speak of killing him. Reuben tries to restrain them from shedding blood. However, he does not talk of the will of God. This is a third time the narrator has not taken an opportunity to speak of God. The Cain and Abel story has already made plain God's horror of fratricide, and the end of the Flood story has condemned in more general terms the taking of human life (Genesis 9.5–6). In the story of Jonah the pagan sailors are frightened to throw the prophet overboard because of how God might react, and, when Jonah insists, pray to God not to hold them guilty of spilling innocent blood (Jonah 1.12–14). Reuben offers no prayer, makes no appeal to God's sensitivities. It is as if God is out of sight and out of mind.

Yet, as it turns out, this chapter deceives us somewhat. God is mentioned three times in chapter 38's story of Tamar and Judah, and nine times in chapter 39, when Joseph returns to the stage. All in all there are over fifty explicit references to God in the Joseph story. Still, however, chapter 37 tells a tale that is true in part. For though God does not remain out of mind, he does stay out of sight, and nearly out of earshot also. There is no equivalent in this end part of Genesis to the story of the meeting with God in the Garden, with which the book nearly began. No daring to teach God how to be God, either. No annunciation in the desert. No wrestling with God through the small, dark hours. Nothing at all so remarkable, nothing so mysterious. Only this:

God spoke to Israel in visions of the night, and said, 'Jacob! Jacob!' He said, 'Here I am.' He said, 'I am God, the God of your father. Do not be afraid to go down to Egypt, for I will set you up as a great nation there. I myself will go down with you to Egypt, and I myself will bring you up, yes, bring you up, and Joseph will lay his hand upon your eyes.' (46.2–4)

The words are hardly insignificant. They remind us of the first promises to Abraham in Genesis 12, and of the assurance God gave Jacob at Beth-El that he would be with him as he journeyed on towards Haran. The double 'Jacob! Jacob!', and his simple reply, 'Here I am' make us think at once of the 'Abraham! Abraham!' ... 'Here I am' of the climax of the Abraham and Isaac story of Genesis 22. The reassurance that God will be in Egypt will gather much extra force when Jacob's descendants find themselves the victims of terrible Egyptian persecution. The promise, made with such insistence, that God will bring Jacob/Israel out of Egypt, will turn out to be a prophecy not just of Jacob's funeral procession to Canaan (Genesis 50.7–13), but of the exodus itself. And God ends here with words that possess the economy and the beauty of the best Hebrew writing, to assure Jacob that his favourite son will be at his deathbed, and will stretch out his hand to close his eyes at death.

There is much to ponder upon here, certainly, yet after the earlier chapters of Genesis we feel there is also much that is missing. There is no drama, no intimacy to astound us, nor any particular daring, and only the beginnings of dialogue. Though God speaks 'in visions of the night', nothing appears to be seen, and the language of seeing seems to have no reality, but to be a mere borrowing from other more lively tales. The double calling of the name lacks the necessary urgency it has in Genesis 22, or will have again in the story of the call of Moses in Exodus 3.4, or of Samuel in 1 Samuel 3.4, 10. That too seems artificial, not demanded by its context, as if God is somehow merely being correct. His words provoke no amazement in Jacob, as did the encounters with him at Beth-El and the Jabbok.

And this small passage is all there is, the only time that God comes out of hiding in the whole of Joseph's story. Nowhere do we hear of Joseph himself, or any of his brothers for that matter, 'seeing' or 'hearing' God. If we ask for a dramatic story of God's encounter with any of them, we are disappointed. We are told four times in the space of a single chapter that God is 'with' Joseph (39.2, 3, 21, 23; see also verse 5). Pharaoh will also describe him as 'one in whom is the spirit of God', a person beyond parallel in wisdom and discernment (41.38–9). Joseph himself will tell Pharaoh that he is only able to interpret his dreams for him through divine inspiration (41.16; see also verses 25 and 28). And later he will take it upon himself to explain the will of God to his brothers (45.5–9; 50.20). But that is as far as these chapters go.

Why is that the case? Why is there nothing more? Is Walter Brueggemann right when he speaks of the Joseph material betraying 'a much more urbane and sophisticated religious perspective (which is not to say superior) in which nothing so direct [as Jacob's encounters with God] ever happens'?[1] Speaking only for myself, I would reject 'sophisticated', but accept 'urbane'. For so long we were brought up in the West to think of stories about God that everyone could engage with as less sophisticated than learned treatises, which were carefully composed in technical terms that only the highly educated and the clever could understand. Over the last nineteen hundred years within the confines of the Christian Church the maker and teacher of doctrine has enjoyed a status and respectability denied to the poet or the storyteller. Even today, you find the occasional biblical scholar who really should know better, writing disparagingly about the stories of the earlier chapters of Genesis, in which God plays such a dramatic part (I do not, of course, include Brueggemann among them; through his writings he has done so much to release their power). The majority, however, have come to a fresh recognition of both the artistry, the power and sheer fascination of those stories, and the sophistication, yes, the sophistication of their way of speaking of God. For some years now I have tried my own hand at writing stories about God,[2] and that has made me see more clearly what these storytellers were up to, and how much more can be said about God and God's world by their means of communication, than through argument and discourse. Along with others,[3] I am at times disturbed by what they say about God, and I have already expressed some of my disquiet in this book, but my admiration for the way they say it only increases each time I turn to their stories and walk their intricate paths.

Yet Brueggemann has a point when he describes the Joseph story as 'urbane'. That word comes from the Latin for city, *urbs*, and indeed the Joseph story moves us from the countryside, where we have been almost throughout the earlier chapters of Genesis, to the city. Nor does it take us to some insignificant, provincial place. Together with Joseph in Egypt, we are in the capital of one of the most advanced and wealthy cultures of the ancient Near East. More importantly, we have entered the world of complex bureaucracy and hierarchy, the world of kings and their courtiers, of wise men celebrated for their wisdom and their cleverness, and of magicians famed for their possession of rare powers (see the reference to the 'magicians and wise men' of Egypt in 41.8). We are in the world of highly organized religion, where the gulf between heaven and earth is not bridged by a stairway busy with heavenly messengers, but by an elite of powerful, *urbane* men. In this world Joseph does astonishingly well, rising from the position of a foreign prisoner who had been charged with sexual assault upon the wife of a high-ranking official, to the second most powerful figure in the land, answerable only to Pharaoh himself!

However, there is a high price to be paid for his success, by the other characters in his story, and even by us, the current readers of it. For he achieves it by evincing, or at least claiming, the ability to read the mind of God *as nobody else can*. The storyteller puts Joseph between us and the God of his story. This Joseph gets in the way of our encountering God for ourselves, for he claims a wisdom and insight for himself which we ordinary mortals do not, and, perhaps, cannot possess. His brothers do not have it, the 'wise men' of Egypt do not have it, even Pharaoh, considered a god by his own people, does not have it. What hope, then, for us? We, together with his brothers and Pharaoh and his court, must rely on Joseph to reveal to us what is going on. He must be the go-between. He must enter the holy of holies for them and for us, that remote place where his God dwells, otherwise inaccessible and incomprehensible. Without him we are left in the darkness of our poor ignorance. He must bring out of God's presence the interpretations of Pharaoh's dreams; he must declare to his brothers and to us the secret of God's activity in the events of his life. Joseph is an expert. We and everyone else, with the possible exception of his father Jacob, are mere fools in his company. Even what he conveys to us is limited. If he has any stories to tell about remarkable encounters of his own with God, he is not sharing them with anyone. We are never taken anywhere near the heart of his religious life.

Joseph is an expert. But is he always *right*? The question is raised most sharply by two speeches of his to his brothers. The first is part of the scene where finally he reveals his identity to them. The second comes at the end of the book, and is his penultimate speech.

'Now do not be hurt, and do not be upset that you sold me here, for it was to save life that God sent me ahead of you. For this is the second year there has been famine deep in the land, and still there are five years to come when there will be no ploughing nor harvest. God sent me ahead of you to set you up as a remnant on earth, and to keep you alive as a great body of survivors. So now, it is not you who sent me here, but God. For he has set me up as a father to Pharaoh, as lord of all his house, and as ruler over the whole of the land of Egypt. (45.5–8)

'Hurry, go up to my father, and say to him, "Thus says your son Joseph. God has set me up as lord of all Egypt. Come down to me. Do not delay. You shall settle in the land of Goshen, and you shall be near me, you, your sons, your sons' sons, your flocks and your herds, and all that you have. I will maintain you there – for there are still five years of famine to come – in case you lose your inheritance, you and your house and all that you have." ' (9–11)

Joseph said to them, 'Do not be afraid, for am I in place of God? You, you planned evil for me. God planned it for good, in order to do as on this day, to keep many people alive. Now do not be afraid. I myself will maintain you and your little ones.' (50.19–21a)

Never mind how we regard the way Joseph treats his brothers here. Never mind if he talks too much. Never mind if we find him patronizing, bearing all the marks of having been too long in power and at the centre of everyone's adulation. What do we make of his theology? On the first passage Karen Armstrong says this:

> Genesis as a whole does not accept this theological view of a wholly omnipotent and irresistible God, in whose grand design human beings are mere pawns. From a very early stage, the biblical authors suggested, God lost control of his creation. He had given humanity free will, and that meant that they shared his sovereign freedom. This alone should make us question Joseph's theology and his interpretation of events.[4]

Her comment on the second passage, the one from Genesis 50, is rather more caustic:

> it has been clear throughout that for all Joseph's talk about God's omnipotence, he really believed that *he* was the one in control.[5]

These statements are fair. God promised Jacob that he would be with him when he went down to Egypt, but Joseph seems to be telling his father that *his* being with him will be enough. He, Joseph, will see to it that he survives and flourishes, and that the ancient promises of God do not fail, and he will look after his brothers and their families in the same way. Human beings are certainly created in Genesis to cooperate with God, and are given the royal power to do it. But this does not mean they have the right to take over

God's role! Assuredly the God of Genesis needs human beings to work with him if his plans for his creation are to succeed. They have the freedom to challenge him, and even give him lessons on how to conduct himself. But they are called to work *with him*, not *instead of him*. Conversely, as Karen Armstrong also points out, they are not created as God's puppets. Only in the Flood are they swept along (and most of them away) by his irresistible power, and as we saw in our chapter on that story, at the end God vows never again to seek such absolute control.[6] William McKane believes that once God recedes into the background of events in Genesis, the human characters have a much greater degree of freedom.[7] Ironically, if Joseph's theology is to be believed, the very reverse is the case.

It is possible, of course, that the theology of the Joseph story is different from the one prevailing in the rest of the book. It is possible, also, that the narrator meant us to take Joseph seriously and trust his judgement. But just as we cannot be sure what was in the narrator's mind, neither can he control how we respond to his story. We might wish to argue that the Joseph story had a different origin from the rest of Genesis, but the fact remains that it is now part of that larger work, and we cannot help but make comparisons with the rest of the material.

So Karen Armstrong's comments are surely justified. We are not only free to question Joseph's interpretation of events; the rest of Genesis invites us to do so. Joseph is not just an expert, but a flawed expert. He is too full of his expertise. He gets in the way. Putting his opulent figure between us and God, he hides him from us and obscures his purposes.

Why then has Joseph been so often held up for our admiration? Because undue admiration is what intermediaries between God and their fellow human beings generally demand, and generally receive. I am a Christian priest (canon of a cathedral, no less!), and some lay people see me as there to act as intermediary between them and God. They can be forgiven for that. They have been brought up to regard all priests in that light, and both the words and the body language of much of the public worship they attend only encourage them to continue to do so. I too can be forgiven, though less easily, if I collude with them, for occupying pedestals can produce a pleasant sense of superiority, and I am only human. But pedestals only make their occupants lonely, big-headed, and misguided: we think we have a clearer view, when in fact we have our heads in the clouds. More seriously still, our supposed superiority denies others their proper status.

Jesus in the Gospels tells his followers they must be prepared to accept the status of a slave, or of a criminal on the way to crucifixion, or of a young child who has no say in the matter of anything. But then the Jesus of the Gospels is no Joseph.

*　　*　　*

What then has happened in Genesis? Is Karen Armstrong again right in her judgement that 'Genesis traces God's gradual disappearance from the human scene'?[8]

In fact, the truth is more complex than that. We saw a particular intimacy between God and human beings in the Garden of Eden, a naturalness of relations there, which are nowhere quite recaptured. With the end of the Cain and Abel story we saw the demise of prayer as conversation. From then onwards even the boldest prayer would carry with it a degree of formality. Too soon, too soon all dialogue with God was washed away in the Flood, and despite the change in God it brought about, the prospect of real intimacy with him seemed lost for ever. Then, however, Abraham came on the scene, and dialogue was restored, and what dialogue! With Abraham relations with God reached at times a new maturity, not glimpsed before. He and God had a great deal to do with one another and a great deal to say to each other. Alas, the stories paid hardly any heed to Sarah and *her* relationship with God, but at least her Egyptian slave, Hagar, twice met God in the desert. She saw him, and heard him, and was changed by him. He paid her some close attention, even if it was not entirely welcome the first time, and he was prepared to enter into dialogue with her. And

Hagar's God went away from the encounter also changed, with a new name, a new identity to be celebrated for years to come at the well of Beer-lahai-roi.

Mixed messages were conveyed by the stories about Jacob that preceded the appearance of Joseph. On the one hand, God was hidden almost entirely from our sight in the opening chapters, until the meeting at Beth-El, and he was again mostly in the wings while Jacob and Laban occupied the stage. On the other hand, he came down to earth on a patch of ground which would for evermore be called Beth-El, the House of God, while at the Jabbok he appeared in human form, a God incarnate, and came as close as any storyteller, as any believer, could imagine.

With the Joseph story that dangerous, will-o'-the-wisp, most intimate, most enthralling God of the Jabbok, the God whom Hagar dared to name, and whom Abraham tried to teach a lesson, that God has disappeared, it is true, but his going has been more sudden than expected.

Some may suppose the narrative is the better for his absence, more realistic, its new world more recognizable and more akin to our own. For God hides in the wings of our story too, it seems, and leaves us to make what sense of things, what sense of him, we can. Yet that is only part of our truth. Another, more disconcerting, but immensely more exciting part is still told by Adam and Eve, by Cain, perhaps by Noah, certainly by Abraham, Hagar and Jacob. Their stories are still, on extraordinary occasions, our stories. And their stories still possess the power to make God real and bring him close. They can still remind us of the naturalness and essential simplicity of prayer, and of the opportunity to engage with God in robust and demanding dialogue. They continue to speak of the possibility of discovering him in the desert when all seems lost. They can make us dream of having him in our grasp, and finding ourselves in his. Stories such as these, and these very stories, can bring us once again to look God in the eye and tell him how it is.

Notes

1 *Meeting God in the Garden*

1. I discuss the portrayal of the woman in the Garden at some length in, Trevor Dennis, *Sarah Laughed: Women's Voices in the Old Testament* (SPCK, 1994), pp. 8–33.
2. I am fully aware of the consensus that has developed in scholarship since the publication of Phyllis Trible's, *God and the Rhetoric of Sexuality* (Fortress Press, 1978), claiming that the *'adam*, the creature made in Genesis 2.7, is not male, but one comprising both male and female. Much as I am attracted to such a reading, I find it difficult to reconcile with Genesis 2.22–3, where God brings the newly created woman to the *'adam*, and the *'adam* exclaims, 'this one will be called "woman" (*'ishshah*), for from *man* (*'ish*) was she taken'. If we were meant to see the *'adam* as comprising both female as well as male, and as 'split' into the two genders at Genesis 2.21–2, then would it not have been the other way round? Would not God have brought the woman to the *man*, the *'ish*, and would not the *'ish* have welcomed her as made like him out of the *'adam*? (Of course, I realize that would have ruined the play on words!) I readily acknowledge, however, that 'man', or 'male' has no meaning without 'woman' and 'female'. That is why, in this part of my discussion, I have avoided the term 'man' till after the woman is created.
3. For the translation, 'side', rather than the traditional, but sadly misguided, 'rib', see Dennis, *Sarah Laughed*, pp. 13–14.
4. For a note on my representing the divine name in this way, see the Introduction, p. xi.
5. Samuel E. Balentine, in *Prayer in the Hebrew Bible: The Drama of the Divine–Human Dialogue* (Fortress Press, 1993), p. 30, shies away from calling it prayer. His judgement of this, and of Cain's dialogue with God in Genesis 4, is 'that they are related to but not identical with prayer'.

94

6. Gordon J. Wenham also comments on the cultic background to this part of the story in his, *Genesis 1—15* (Word Biblical Commentary, Word Publishing, 1987), p. 86.

7. In the temple rebuilt in Jerusalem after the exile, when the monarchy was no more, the Holy of Holies was entered but once a year by the High Priest on the Day of Atonement, but the Eden story may well predate such an exclusive practice as that.

2 In a Field Howling with a Brother's Blood

1. The women in the Garden, Sarah, at Genesis 18.15, Rebekah, at 25.22, and Rachel, at 30.6, have brief dealings with God, and there are Hagar's encounters with him in 16.7–13 and 21.15–19 (those last two passages are discussed below in Chapter 5). But these are the only exceptions in Genesis.

2. 'The Story of Cain and Abel: A Narrative Study', *JSOT* 52 (1991), p. 39; see also her book, *Stories of the Beginning: Genesis 1—11 and Other Creation Stories* (SCM, 1996), pp. 85–6.

3. For the translation, 'the sin of lying in wait', behind which lies a single Hebrew word, I am indebted to Ellen van Wolde. See, 'The Story of Cain and Abel', pp. 31–2. Her whole discussion of the translation and interpretation of 4.6–7 (see pp. 29–32 of her article) is most interesting.

4. The Hebrew term for 'longing' in 4.7 is extremely rare. It is found in only two other places in the Old Testament, in Genesis 3.16, and in The Song of Songs 7.10.

5. See van Wolde, 'The Story of Cain and Abel', p. 35.

6. The Hebrew here is ambiguous. This is a perfectly possible interpretation of it, particularly given the curse put on the ground in 3.17. Alternatively, Pride-and-joy could be cursed from the ground, meaning that his ability to work the ground and gain a living from it is destroyed. Either way the link between him and the ground is effectively broken. It will not even yield thorns and thistles to him any more.

3 Only the Sound of Rain

1. Most translations speak of the woman's 'pain' in 3.16, but, in fact, the same word is applied to her in the Hebrew as is used in the

very next verse of the man's back-breaking labour in the fields. See my discussion in *Sarah Laughed*, pp. 26–7.

2. The same word in the Hebrew is used both at the end of 6.12 to describe the state of the earth before the Flood, and in 6.13 and 6.17 to describe what God intends to do to it.

3. Claus Westermann, *Genesis 1—11: A Commentary* (SPCK, 1984), pp. 393–4.

4. In the case of 8.21, the versions are divided. The RSV, for example, the NRSV, the JB and NJB are all on the side of 'because', while the NEB, the REB, the NIV would support 'though'.

5. Wenham, *Genesis 1—15*, pp. 165–6, contrasts the portrayal of Noah with that of Utnapishtim in the Epic of Gilgamesh, one of the ancient Flood stories which was a significant source for the Genesis story.

4 Telling God how to be God

1. I discuss this passage at some length in *Sarah Laughed*, pp. 47–52.

2. Alas, the reading finds some support in the New Testament, at 2 Peter 2.6–10 and Jude 7.

3. See the very illuminating article by Ken Stone, 'Gender and Homosexuality in Judges 19: Subject – Honor, Object – Shame?', *JSOT* 67 (1995), pp. 87–107. There are significant parallels between Judges 19 and Genesis 19, and Stone throws considerable light on the Genesis passage.

4. See Ernst Wurthwein, *The Text of the Old Testament: An Introduction to the Biblia Hebraica* (SCM, 1979), pp. 18–19. To their credit, the New Jerusalem Bible, with its, 'Yahweh remained in Abraham's presence', and the Good News Bible, with, 'but the Lord remained with Abraham', both respect the textual critics' arguments, even if their translations are a trifle too cautious.

5. See Isaiah 29.16; 45.9–13 (and Romans 9.20, where Paul draws upon the Isaiah passages to make his own point).

6. This, and Genesis 19.13, are the only places where the Hebrew term for 'outcry' is used in this way. Normally it is applied to the cries of distress of the victim, not to the clamour of the perpetrators of violence.

7. Such is the immediate sense of the term used in the Hebrew: see Walter Brueggemann, *Genesis (Interpretation* Commentary, John

Knox Press, 1982), p. 171. He calls the standard translation of 18.25, 'Far be it from you to do such a thing', 'weak and misleading'. Mary Korsak gives the translation, 'Profanation!' in her 1992 translation of Genesis, Mary Korsak, *At the start ...* (Leuvense Schrijversaktie, 1992), p. 59.

8. Abraham is actually called God's 'friend' in Isaiah 41.8 and 2 Chronicles 20.7. See also James 2.23.

5 Naming the Unnameable

1. I have treated the Hagar stories also in *Sarah Laughed*, ch. 3 (and see also ch. 2), but I come at them this time with fresh concerns, and produce, I hope, fresh insights.

2. Phyllis Trible, *Texts of Terror: Literary-Feminist Readings of Biblical Narratives* (Fortress Press, 1984), p. 28.

3. S. J. Teubal, *Hagar the Egyptian: The Lost Traditions of the Matriarchs* (Harper and Row, 1990), pp. 191–200, reprinted in Athalya Brenner (ed.), *A Feminist Companion to Genesis* (Sheffield Academic Press, 1993), pp. 235–50.

4. See above, p. 10; also my *Sarah Laughed*, pp. 124, 178–9.

5. Though see my discussion of 16.2 in *Sarah Laughed*, p. 43.

6. See Genesis 12.10–20, and my comment upon that passage in *Sarah Laughed*, pp. 37–40.

7. Claus Westermann, *Genesis 12—36: A Commentary* (SPCK, 1985), p. 246.

8. Stephen Mitchell, *The Book of Job* (North Point Press, 1979), p. 79.

9. See Teubal, *Hagar the Egyptian*, in Brenner (ed.), *A Feminist Companion to Genesis*, pp. 236–7.

10. See Arie Troost, 'Reading for the Author's Signature: Genesis 21.1–21 and Luke 15.11–32 as Intertexts', in Brenner (ed.), *A Feminist Companion to Genesis*, pp. 261–3.

6 God in the Dark

1. There is another reading of that episode which turns Isaac into the trickster and leaves him much more in control of events. See Adrien Janis Bledstein, 'Binder, Trickster, Heel and Hairy-Man: Rereading Genesis 27 as a Trickster Tale Told by a Woman', in Brenner (ed.), *A Feminist Companion to Genesis*, pp. 282–95.

2. See John L. McKenzie, 'Jacob at Peniel: Genesis 32.24–32', *CBQ* 25 (1963), pp. 71–6, and Heather A. McKay, 'Jacob Makes it across the Jabbok', *JSOT* 38 (1987), p. 4.
3. Though Bledstein, in her article on Genesis 27 (see above, note 1), hears the voice of a female storyteller in that chapter.
4. For these plays on words, and others in this passage, and the 'dance' they create, see Jan P. Fokkelman, *Narrative Art in Genesis: Specimens of Stylistic and Structural Analysis*, 2nd edn (JSOT Press, 1991), pp. 66–73. That whole chapter of Fokkelman's book (pp. 46–81; see also pp. 121–2) is devoted to this passage in Genesis, and is well worth careful study.
5. See Trevor Dennis, *Lo and Behold! The Power of Old Testament Storytelling* (SPCK, 1991), pp. 56–7.
6. McKay, 'Jacob Makes it across the Jabbok', p. 9.
7. Genesis offers two interpretations of the name 'Jacob'. In 25.26 it is linked to the Hebrew word for heel, *'aqeb*, in 27.36 with the verb *'aqab*, meaning to cheat. 'Heel-catcher' is Fokkelman's clever attempt to combine both meanings (see *Narrative Art*, p. 215).
8. Fokelmann, *Narrative Art*, p. 188.
9. *Narrative Art*, pp. 212–13.
10. Hermann Gunkel, *The Folktale in the Old Testament* (The Almond Press, 1987), p. 84. (Gunkel's book first appeared in German in 1917.)
11. I explored the notion of such a background in *Lo and Behold!*, pp. 49–53.
12. See Gerhard von Rad, *Genesis*, OTL Commentary, 2nd edn (SCM, 1963), p. 280.
13. See also Judges 6.22; 13.22–3.
14. *Narrative Art*, p. 215.

7 *An Expert Intervenes*

1. Brueggemann, *Genesis*, pp. 353–4.
2. I have two small collections of stories published: *Speaking of God: A Collection of Stories* (Triangle, 1992); *Imagining God: Stories from Creation to Heaven* (SPCK, 1997).
3. There is an increasing and welcome tendency in current scholarship to face the limitations and flaws of the theology of the Genesis stories and other such OT material. See, for example:

David J. A. Clines, *Interested Parties: The Ideology of Writers and Readers of the Hebrew Bible* (Sheffield Academic Press, 1995); Karen Armstrong, *In the Beginning: A New Reading of the Book of Genesis* (HarperCollins, 1996); R. N. Whybray, 'The Immorality of God: Reflections on some Passages in Genesis, Job, Exodus and Numbers', *JSOT* 72 (1996), pp. 89–120. Their comment, born out of a passionate interest in the text and painstaking study of it, has nothing to do, of course, with the easy dismissal of 'the God of the Old Testament' we come across in some Christian sermons or writings.

4. Armstrong, *In the Beginning*, p. 113.
5. *In the Beginning*, p. 114.
6. See above pp. 31–2.
7. William McKane, *Studies in the Patriarchal Narratives* (Handsel Press, 1979), p. 240; see also p. 43.
8. Armstrong, *In the Beginning*, pp. 118–19.

References

Armstrong, Karen, *In the Beginning: A New Reading of the Book of Genesis*, HarperCollins, 1996

Balentine, Samuel E., *Prayer in the Hebrew Bible: The Drama of the Divine–Human Dialogue*, Fortress Press, 1993

Bledstein, Adrien Janis, 'Binder, Trickster, Heel and Hairy-Man: Rereading Genesis 27 as a Trickster Tale Told by a Woman', in Athalya Brenner (ed.), *A Feminist Companion to Genesis*, Sheffield Academic Press, 1993

Brueggemann, Walter, *Genesis*, *Interpretation* Commentary, John Knox Press, 1982

Clines, David J. A., *Interested Parties: The Ideology of Writers and Readers of the Hebrew Bible*, Sheffield Academic Press, 1995

Dennis, Trevor, *Lo and Behold! The Power of Old Testament Storytelling*, SPCK, 1991

Dennis, Trevor, *Speaking of God: A Collection of Stories*, Triangle, 1992

Dennis, Trevor, *Sarah Laughed: Women's Voices in the Old Testament*, SPCK, 1994

Dennis, Trevor, *Imagining God: Stories from Creation to Heaven*, SPCK, 1997

Fokkelman, J. P., *Narrative Art in Genesis: Specimens of Stylistic and Structural Analysis*, 2nd edn., JSOT Press, 1991

Gunkel, Hermann, *The Folktale in the Old Testament*, Almond Press, 1987

Korsak, Mary, *At the start . . .* , Leuvense Schrijversaktie, 1992

McKane, William, *Studies in the Patriarchal Narratives*, Handsel Press, 1979

McKay, Heather A., 'Jacob Makes it across the Jabbok', *JSOT* 38 (1987)

McKenzie, John L., 'Jacob at Peniel: Genesis 32.24–32', *CBQ* 25 (1963)

Mitchell, Stephen, *The Book of Job*, North Point Press, 1979

Rad, Gerhard von, *Genesis*, OTL Commentary, 2nd edn, SCM, 1963

Stone, Ken, 'Gender and Homosexuality in Judges 19: Subject – Honor, Object – Shame?', *JSOT* 67 (1995)

Teubal, S. J., *Hagar the Egyptian: The Lost Traditions of the Matriarchs*, Harper and Row, 1990, reprinted in Athalya Brenner (ed.), *A Feminist Companion to Genesis*, Sheffield Academic Press, 1993

Trible, Phyllis, *God and the Rhetoric of Sexuality*, Fortress Press, 1978

Trible, Phyllis, *Texts of Terror: Literary-Feminist Readings of Biblical Narratives*, Fortress Press, 1984

Troost, Arie, 'Reading for the Author's Signature: Genesis 21.1–21 and Luke 15.11–32 as Intertexts', in Athalya Brenner (ed.), *A Feminist Companion to Genesis*, Sheffield Academic Press, 1993

Wenham, Gordon J., *Genesis 1—15*, Word Biblical Commentary, Word Publishing, 1987

Westermann, Claus, *Genesis 1—11: A Commentary*, SPCK, 1984

Westermann, Claus, *Genesis 12—36: A Commentary*, SPCK, 1985

Whybray, R. N., 'The Immorality of God: Reflections on some Passages in Genesis, Job, Exodus and Numbers', *JSOT* 72 (1996)

Wolde, Ellen van, 'The Story of Cain and Abel: A Narrative Study', *JSOT* 52 (1991)

Wolde, Ellen van, *Stories of the Beginning: Genesis 1—11 and Other Creation Stories*, SCM, 1996

Wurthwein, Ernst, *The Text of the Old Testament: an Introduction to the Biblia Hebraica*, SCM, 1979

Index

Bible Reference Index